Heywood Walter Seton Karr

Shores and Alps of Alaska

Heywood Walter Seton Karr

Shores and Alps of Alaska

ISBN/EAN: 9783337127497

Printed in Europe, USA, Canada, Australia, Japan

Cover: Foto ©Andreas Hilbeck / pixelio.de

More available books at **www.hansebooks.com**

SHORES AND ALPS

OF

ALASKA

BY

H. W. SETON KARR, F.R.G.S.
ETC.

With Illustrations and Two Maps

LONDON:
SAMPSON LOW, MARSTON, SEARLE, & RIVINGTON,
CROWN BUILDINGS, 188 FLEET STREET, E.C.
1887

PREFACE.

THE clearest and simplest manner of describing a journey of exploration, of sport, or of adventure, is often in the form of the original diary—penned *in situ* from day to day in the tent, the forest, or the canoe, on the shore, the glacier, or the mountain side. Such a book does this profess to be, having the merits, if it has the defects, of an instantaneous word-photograph, rather than of a carefully elaborated work of art.

When, as the *New York Times* Expedition to Alaska, and as the first explorers who had ever landed on that stern coast, we made our attempt upon Mount St. Elias, our combined *alpinism* was insignificant. Our experience had been gleaned from divers places. Lieutenant Schwatka had travelled in the Arctic, Professor Libbey in Colorado, and the writer had mountaineered in the Alps. An expedition comprising Swiss guides, or consisting of experienced climbers, would be more successful.

The interior of the mysterious Kenai Peninsula, and the regions between the Yukon River and Cook's Inlet, are as yet unknown and unexplored, with the exception of the Tannanah, which was descended by Lieutenant Allen.

As the first explorer in the footsteps of Cook to make the circuit of the coast northwards from Cape Spencer, or the canoe journey from Kaiak to Prince William Sound, the writer has attempted to describe a country which will soon become better known.

CONTENTS.

INTRODUCTION.

FROM THE ATLANTIC TO THE PACIFIC BY THE NEW RAILWAY ACROSS THE ROCKY MOUNTAINS.

Winnipeg—Medicine Hat—The Buffalo extinct—Calgary and Fort Macleod—The Cattle-ranching Industry—An Excursion to the Canadian National Park—The Hot Springs—Alone at Devil's Lake—The Peaks near the Kicking Horse—Golden City—The Big Bend—Peaks of the Selkirks—Rogers Pass—The Loops—Second Crossing of the Columbia—Western Notices—Over the Eagle—We travel on a Handcar—Forest Fires—Shuswap Lake—The Farming Country—Kamloops Lake—Cañons of the Thompson and the Fraser—Off for Alaska—The *New York Times* Expedition—Game and Aspects of Vancouver Island—The Early Navigators—Nanaimo — Esquimault — The Indians — The Chinese — Climate of Victoria—Elk, Blacktail, Salmon-trout, and Mountain Goats 1

CHAPTER I.

Northwards from Victoria—The Great Sea-River, or the Inland Passage—Nanaimo—Tongass—Metlakatla—The Skeena River—Cape Fox—Loring—Wrangel—The Taku Inlet—Juneau—Chilcat and Chilcoot—Glacier Bay—Muir's Glacier—Sitka or New Archangel—A Fishing and Shooting Excursion—The Fourth of July at Sitka 25

CHAPTER II.

From Sitka to the Alaskan Alps—The U.S.S. *Pinta*—Mount Fairweather—Arrival at Yakatat—The Mount St. Elias range—The Yakatat Indians—The Swedish Traders—Indian Curiosities—The Man-o'-War at the Village—Interviews with the Chief 45

CHAPTER III.

We leave Yakatat for Icy Bay—Landing in the Surf—The Base Camp—Strawberries and Bear-Trails—The Start for Mount St. Elias—Fording a Glacial Torrent—A Mighty Stream—The Quicksands—A Mountainous Moraine Overgrown with Forest—An Ice-buried River 62

CHAPTER IV.

Waiting by the Ice—The Indians Return for more Provisions—A vast Moraine overgrown with Trees and Resting upon Moving Ice—Parted from the Guides—Stopped by a Lake of Bergs—We Separate to find a Way—A Dammed-up Torrent Breaks out afresh—Gradual Burial of a Forest Island—Loss of the Professor—Fire, Ice, and Water—We Start again—More Glacial Lakes and the Great Tyndall Glacier—The Fifth Camp reached—Preparations for the Final Ascent 83

CHAPTER V.

The Ascent of Mount St. Elias—Dangerous Crevasses—We are Roped—The Ascent—I reach 6800 Feet over Snow-line—A Bear close to Camp—A Description of the Mountain—The Return to Icy Bay—Quicksands—Three Bears Killed—An Attempt to Launch our Whaleboat through the Surf—We Swamp at Midnight 101

CHAPTER VI.

A Fresh Attempt to Pass the Surf of Icy Bay—Abandonment of our Possessions—Skirting the Shore—Crossing Yakatat Bay—We camp by the Indian Village—Haggling with the Natives, or "Chin-music"—Our Life at Yakatat—An Attempt to Recover the Abandoned Property—The Kaiak Traders arrive in their Schooner—Poisoning of the Indians with Arsenic—Murder of George Holt—The Chief Medicine-Man—I leave Yakatat—The *New York Times* Expedition waits for the Man-o'-War—Becalmed—Shooting Seals—A Sea-otter Hunt—Cape Yagtag—A Wild Stern Coast-line—Another enormous Glacier—Life on the Schooner—Cape Suckling—Cape Martin—Kaiak Island 119

CONTENTS.

INTRODUCTION.

FROM THE ATLANTIC TO THE PACIFIC BY THE NEW RAILWAY ACROSS THE ROCKY MOUNTAINS.

Winnipeg—Medicine Hat—The Buffalo extinct—Calgary and Fort Macleod—The Cattle-ranching Industry—An Excursion to the Canadian National Park—The Hot Springs—Alone at Devil's Lake—The Peaks near the Kicking Horse—Golden City—The Big Bend—Peaks of the Selkirks—Rogers Pass—The Loops—Second Crossing of the Columbia—Western Notices—Over the Eagle—We travel on a Handcar—Forest Fires—Shuswap Lake—The Farming Country—Kamloops Lake—Cañons of the Thompson and the Fraser—Off for Alaska—The *New York Times* Expedition—Game and Aspects of Vancouver Island—The Early Navigators—Nanaimo — Esquimault — The Indians — The Chinese — Climate of Victoria—Elk, Blacktail, Salmon-trout, and Mountain Goats 1

CHAPTER I.

Northwards from Victoria—The Great Sea-River, or the Inland Passage—Nanaimo—Tongass—Metlakatla—The Skeena River—Cape Fox—Loring—Wrangel—The Taku Inlet—Juneau—Chilcat and Chilcoot—Glacier Bay—Muir's Glacier—Sitka or New Archangel—A Fishing and Shooting Excursion—The Fourth of July at Sitka 25

CHAPTER II.

From Sitka to the Alaskan Alps—The U.S.S. *Pinta*—Mount Fairweather—Arrival at Yakatat—The Mount St. Elias range—The Yakatat Indians—The Swedish Traders—Indian Curiosities—The Man-o'-War at the Village—Interviews with the Chief 45

CHAPTER III.

We leave Yakatat for Icy Bay—Landing in the Surf—The Base Camp—Strawberries and Bear-Trails—The Start for Mount St. Elias—Fording a Glacial Torrent—A Mighty Stream—The Quicksands—A Mountainous Moraine Overgrown with Forest—An Ice-buried River 62

CHAPTER IV.

Waiting by the Ice—The Indians Return for more Provisions—A vast Moraine overgrown with Trees and Resting upon Moving Ice—Parted from the Guides—Stopped by a Lake of Bergs—We Separate to find a Way—A Dammed-up Torrent Breaks out afresh—Gradual Burial of a Forest Island—Loss of the Professor—Fire, Ice, and Water—We Start again—More Glacial Lakes and the Great Tyndall Glacier—The Fifth Camp reached—Preparations for the Final Ascent 83

CHAPTER V.

The Ascent of Mount St. Elias—Dangerous Crevasses—We are Roped—The Ascent—I reach 6800 Feet over Snow-line—A Bear close to Camp—A Description of the Mountain—The Return to Icy Bay—Quicksands—Three Bears Killed—An Attempt to Launch our Whaleboat through the Surf—We Swamp at Midnight 101

CHAPTER VI.

A Fresh Attempt to Pass the Surf of Icy Bay—Abandonment of our Possessions—Skirting the Shore—Crossing Yakatat Bay—We camp by the Indian Village—Haggling with the Natives, or "Chin-music"—Our Life at Yakatat—An Attempt to Recover the Abandoned Property—The Kaiak Traders arrive in their Schooner—Poisoning of the Indians with Arsenic—Murder of George Holt—The Chief Medicine-Man—I leave Yakatat—The *New York Times* Expedition waits for the Man-o'-War—Becalmed—Shooting Seals—A Sea-otter Hunt—Cape Yagtag—A Wild Stern Coast-line—Another enormous Glacier—Life on the Schooner—Cape Suckling—Cape Martin—Kaiak Island 119

CHAPTER VII.

Arrival at Kaiak—I become a Naval Officer—Hauling in Dog-Fish—The Hunter's Home and the Indian Village—The Tame Bear—Two Norwegians on Cape Suckling—How the Bear came for them—The Habits of the Sea-Otter—Visiting the Indian Hovels—I become an Admiral, and the Chief is presented to me—The Weather changes 144

CHAPTER VIII.

We are forced to stop at Martin Point—Raw Salmons' Noses—A Bear shot—A Drunken Indian Village—Sliding over the Mud of the Copper River Delta—The Squaw kills a Salmon—Camp on an Island—Estuary of the Copper River—Camp on Hawkins Islands—The Indians Washing—Caught in a Gale—Salmon-fishing Extraordinary—Description of an Alaskan Scene—Captain Cook in Prince William Sound—We arrive at Nuchuk 162

CHAPTER IX.

Our Life at Nuchuk—A Native Ball—The Natives start on a Sea-Otter Hunt in Bidarkies—Description of a Bidarky—Climbing after Grouse—Millions of Salmon—Spearing and Hooking them—Salmon-Drying—Our Russian Bath—A Description of Nuchuk and the Game and Food of Prince William Sound—How the Natives Live, and how the Alaska Commercial Company of San Francisco Trades with them—The Natives as Captain Cook found them . . . 182

CHAPTER X.

Life with the Indians on the Copper River 200

CHAPTER XI.

Waiting at Nuchuk in Prince William Sound—The Indians refuse to move—We prepare to Winter there—The First Snow—Sport at Nuchuk—The Ducks, Grouse, and Geese—The Schooner arrives at last—Chenega and the Coast of the Kenai Peninsula—A Gale—We reach Kodiak—Fearful Murder at our Supper-table—A Terrible Passage to San Francisco—Homewards again . . . , . . 222

APPENDIX.

The Fur Trade of Alaska—Fur-seals—Hair-seals—Sea-Lions—Sea-otters—Prospects of the Fur Trade a Century ago as estimated by Cook—The Varieties of Foxes—Black and Brown Bears—Their Pursuit—The Lynx, Polar Bear, Marten, Cariboo, Moose, Sheep, and Goat—Prince William Sound and its Indians—A Description of Cook's Inlet and its Shores—The Fur-trading Stores—The Volcanoes—Cape Douglas — A Description of the Alaskan Peninsula, its Settlements, Game, and Mountains—Unexplored Alaska—Future Sporting Expeditions—A Chugamute Vocabulary . 234

LIST OF ILLUSTRATIONS.

	PAGE
Mount St. Elias, nearly 20,000 feet in height; from Yakatat Bay, distant over fifty miles (*Frontispiece*).	
The Pass across the Rocky Mountains	4
The Devil's Lake	6
Castle Mountain and the Canadian National Park . .	8
The View from the Hot Springs	8
Cathedral Mountain	10
Crossing the Selkirks; the Source of the Illecillewaet and the first Glacier near the summit of the Rogers Pass . .	13
Rooms to Let	15
How we crossed the Eagle Pass over the Gold Range, on the Canadian Pacific Railway, British Columbia . .	16
Yale, the Gateway to the Cañons of the Fraser . .	18
Nanaimo	20
Indian Tlinkit Carvings on the Pacific Coast . .	21
Stopping to Coal at Nanaimo, Vancouver's Island . .	26
An Indian Totem Pole at Fort Wrangel . . .	27
At Howkan	31
Taku Inlet	33
The Gold Mine on Douglas Island	34
Chilcat	35
Eagle Glacier	36
Davidson Glacier	37
Sitka and Mount Edgcumbe	39
A Young Bear for Five Dollars	40
He "means business, though it is all for pleasure" . .	41
Blacktail	42
The Final Heat	43
The Judge practises the Chinook Language . . .	44
Mount Fairweather, rising to 15,500 feet above the North Pacific Ocean at its base	47
Mount Vancouver, 13,100 feet	51
The Village of the Yakatat Indians	53
Spirit Masks from the Yakatat Indian Sorcerer's Grave .	57
The Start for Mount St. Elias	73
Mount Cook, 16,000 feet, from the Tyndall Glacier .	99
Trying to ascend Mount St. Elias	102
The Professor	126

LIST OF ILLUSTRATIONS.

	PAGE
A Yakatat Medicine Man	129
The St. Elias Alps, the third highest range in the world, viewed from the westward	141
Cape St. Elias	142
The schooner *Three Brothers*	145
Kaiak	147
Indian Hovels at Kaiak	157
Klok-Shegees in his "Store" Clothing	159
At Martin Point	163
August 22d, 5 A.M., looking north-west	169
A Man of Oodiak	170
August 22d, 1 P.M.	171
How the Trees grow in Alaska	173
Nuchuk—The Baidars or Baiderars of the Copper River Indians	183
Nuchuk—The Russian Church	184
Bidarkies	185
A Dog-Salmon	191
Jawbone of a Dog-Salmon	192
Nuchuk—Our Home for Two Months	193
Prince William Sound, Alaska, with Nuchuk Harbour	194
A Man of Oodiak	195
An Alaskan Indian Halibut Hook	196
At Nuchuk—Gustia, once a Slave-Boy	223
Sett-Shoo, a Boy of Oodiak	225
Knight's Island, from five miles north of Chenega, looking east	227
Part of the Kenai Peninsula, from Chenega	228

MAPS AND PLANS.

General Map of Alaska and British Columbia, showing the Author's Route.	
Plan of the Route taken by the *New York Times* Expedition from Icy Bay to Mount St. Elias and back	87
Map of Alaska, from Unpublished Sources, showing Volcanoes, Fur-trading Stations, Indian Villages, and Game Districts	237

From the land of the aurora,
Land untrodden by explorer,
Land of mystery and terror,
Peaks unscaled and seas unfathomed;
From the land of seal and otter,
Land of ptarmigan and penguin,
Land of white wolf and of walrus,
Land of silver fox and ermine,
Land of Yukon, land of Thlinkit,
Land of avalanche and glacier,
Land of midnight sun and silence,
Came a strange and thrilling story;
Came a story of the battle
With the iceberg and the tempest,
With the torrent and the breaker,
With the storm cloud and the north wind
Howling wolf-life through the gorges;
Came the story of the secrets
Wrested from the sullen river,
Wrested from the gloomy mountain,
From the forest and the chasms,
Secrets locked away for ages;
Came this legend, strange and simple,
Full of promise, full of treasure
For the unborn generation;
Came this legend of achievement
In the mighty land—ALASKA.
New York Times.

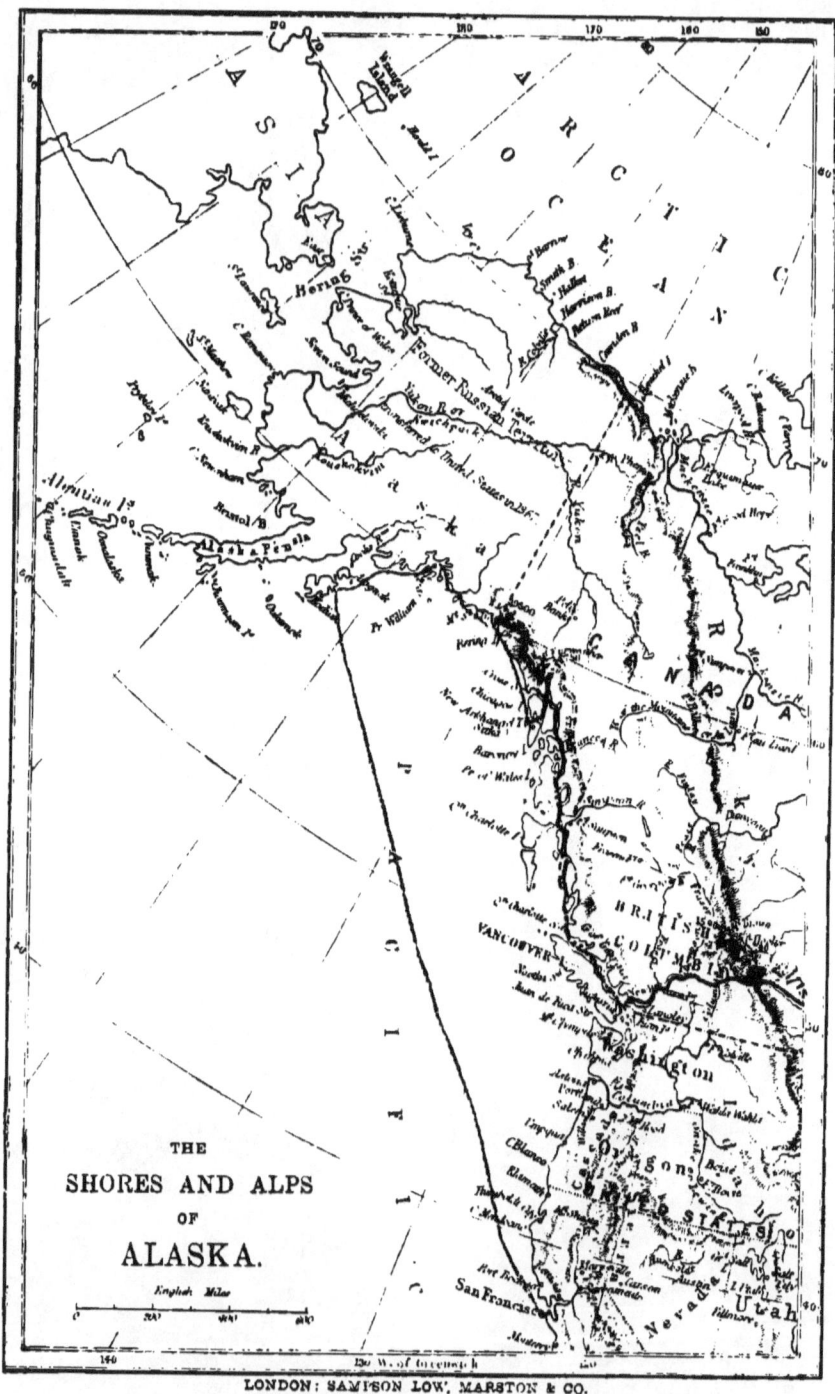

THE
SHORES AND ALPS
OF
ALASKA.

English Miles

LONDON: SAMPSON LOW, MARSTON & CO.

SHORES AND ALPS OF ALASKA.

INTRODUCTION.

FROM THE ATLANTIC TO THE PACIFIC BY THE NEW RAILWAY ACROSS THE ROCKY MOUNTAINS.

Winnipeg—Medicine Hat—The Buffalo extinct—Calgary and Fort Macleod—The Cattle-ranching Industry—An Excursion to the Canadian National Park—The Hot Springs—Alone at Devil's Lake—The Peaks near the Kicking Horse—Golden City—The Big Bend—Peaks of the Selkirks—Rogers Pass—The Loops—Second Crossing of the Columbia—Western Notices—Over the Eagle—We travel on a Hand-car—Forest Fires—Shuswap Lake—The Farming Country—Kamloops Lake—Cañons of the Thompson and the Fraser—Off for Alaska—The *New York Times* Expedition—Game and Aspects of Vancouver Island—The Early Navigators—Nanaimo—Esquimault—The Indians—The Chinese—Climate of Victoria—Elk, Blacktail, Salmon-trout, and Mountain Goats.

ABOARD *The Ancon* (bound for SITKA, ALASKA), *June* 17*th*, 1886.

WE have just completed our journey from the Atlantic to the Pacific Ocean, as some of the very first through passengers by the new Canadian Pacific Railway. It has occupied nearly one month, partly because the line is not yet completely "opened up" for traffic across the mountains; there is still a gap of some miles near the summit of the Eagle Pass (over the Gold or Coast range), which we traversed on a "hand-car." Four thousand men are still working upon the Rogers Pass (over the Selkirk range), and the portion of the line from Kamloops westward to the sea has not yet been "given over" by the contractor, who is, however, running passenger trains over it. But in a few weeks the continent can be crossed from Montreal to Vancouver in five days and fourteen hours, and this will be further reduced to a five days' transit. It will be the longest journey known on any railway in the world (2900 miles).

After leaving Montreal the line passes through a wooded country by Lake Nipissing and the northern rocky shores of Lakes Huron and Superior to Winnipeg. The latter lies at the edge of the more thickly timbered country. From this point, the broad and almost level and treeless prairie stretches westward to the base of the Rocky Mountains. This great mountain-range approaches nearer the Pacific coast in British Columbia than is the case in the States; nor are there in the former such extensive foothills on its eastern slopes. Hence, as we approached Calgary and left the level plains for the most part behind us, the Rockies rose suddenly and more markedly from the table-lands, which are 1300 miles in breadth.

Westward from Regina little of interest is passed, the most important places being Moose-jaw (the abbreviation of a long Indian name), and Medicine Hat (after an Indian conjuror), generally called "The Hat." The country gradually changes from a desolate region of poor lands to a good ranching and cattle-breeding prairie reaching to the very foot of the Rockies. The surface is still covered with trails and the whitening bones of buffaloes. The collection of the latter forms quite an industry. It is but a few years since this region was alive with the buffalo in the herds of thousands; the price offered for their hides has been the cause of their extermination by Indian and white hunters.

I stayed some days at Calgary, the chief town of Alberta, while L. and F. drove south to Fort Macleod. Calgary and Fort Macleod are the head-centres of the great cattle ranches and stock-raising industry of Canada. The extensive Indian reserves which the Government has to supply with beef (in place of the buffalo, now no more in existence), form a good local market.

The public lands are leased as cattle ranches on

liberal terms. One hundred thousand acres can be included in a single lease at two cents an acre for twenty-one years. The best grass is found here and the purest water of any of the cattle-raising districts of the west.

Though only two years old, Calgary boasts two mayors and two rival town councils. We had expected to find some trout-fishing in the Bow

The Pass across the Rocky Mountains.

river, but the water is discoloured and thick from June till September from the melting snows.

A couple of days after arriving, I had the opportunity of joining the "first excursion ever offered to the people of Alberta" to the proposed "Canadian National Park" in the heart of the Rocky Mountains.

From Calgary the line follows the course of the

Bow river as it issues from the portals of the range, to its source near the summit of the Kicking Horse Pass. Jagged and scarred as are the high mountains on either side of the valley of the Bow, yet they give the impression of having been turned out of Dame Nature's workshop only just long enough to allow the pines to grow upon their steep slopes. Never were strata left contorted with such regular irregularity, or mountains formed which gave evidence of such terrifying convulsions, for they stand in regular rows of cliffs and pinnacles.

It was the Queen's birthday. We swept along at a rate of thirty miles an hour through wild rocky scenery, stationed upon a kind of open "Observation car," together with the brass band, which played selections as we proceeded.

As seen from Calgary the range seems broken into the most fantastic shapes, from The Devil's Head in the north (which resembles the Matterhorn with the top broken off) to Mount Head in the south.

It was said that when the summit of The Devil's Head should fall (which has occurred), the country would pass from the possession of the Stony Indians into that of the white man.

The people of this tribe are described as reliable

and honest; they have their villages at Morley, and are expert as hunters and mountaineers. They had just departed for their summer's hunting trip, or we should have taken a couple of them with us.

Almost within sight of Calgary lies the Gap, as the gateway into the mountain valley of the Bow is named. The bold and eccentric contours of the

The Devil's Lake.

mountain walls on either hand increase as one advances nearer to the summit of the Pass.

At Banff I remained till joined by L. and F., camping some miles off at The Devil's Lake for four days entirely alone.

The Rocky Mountains do not on the whole offer good trout-fishing. The Bow river from June till August is charged with muddy snow-water. However, as every one agreed that at The Devil's Lake the water would be clear, and that it was surrounded by high mountains rarely visited and never ascended, I decided to visit it, and got a man and a pack-horse to deposit me there after a dangerous crossing of the swollen Devil's Creek.

No ripple either of breeze or moving fin* broke the glassy surface of The Devil's Lake, which reflected the mountains round in water of such a deep azure blue, as to be almost sufficiently uncanny to account for its name, without taking into consideration the gloomy precipices which overhang its sides.

In front of my tent by the edge of the lake stood, or rather tottered, a withered tree which might have been the veritable Upas Tree, for not a living thing was discernible around.

Only the curious cries of a few wild-fowl broke the silence of the nights, sounding almost human, like preconcerted signals of Indians to attack the camp of the solitary white man. Once or twice a humming-bird hovered and poised itself overhead, and then darted away, startling me with the sudden noise of its wings.

From a summit five thousand feet above the lake

* Later in the season a 27 lb. trout was caught.

an extensive panorama was visible of the Rocky Mountains, two of the peaks being counterparts of the Schreckhorn and Finsteraarhorn.

Castle Mountain and The Canadian National Park.

Bears are unusually numerous this season, and have been seen lately near both of the hot springs in the Park; and on one occasion by some ladies

The View from the Hot Springs.

who are camping near the upper springs, and who informed me that they were much terrified, and had discontinued their walks in the neighbourhood.

The attractions of the district, without in any way rivalling the American Yellowstone National Park, consist, in addition to the mountain scenery, which is remarkable, of two sets of warm springs and of some falls or rapids of the Bow river. The more elevated of the springs command a wide view, while the lower ones are more curious in character. The largest is entirely subterranean, in a dome-shaped cavern which one enters by means of a ladder from the summit. On the floor is a pool with a sandy bottom through which the warm waters bubble up. When one's eyes get accustomed to the gloom it can be seen that the water makes its exit as mysteriously as it entered.

At first I was alone; but afterwards a rough-looking man made his appearance, and offered to take charge of my rifle while I descended. It was thought well to decline.

In full view from Banff on the south side lies Castle Mountain, or Cascade Peak; castellated terraces of rock encircle its summit like impassable walls.

Higher yet lie Mounts Lefroy, Stephen and Hector, and Goat Peak; and on the north a curious rocky fortress guards the summit of the Pass—Cathedral Mountain.

After The Devil's Lake our next camping-place was to be Golden City, where we were to find the small steamer which has been started on the Columbia by an enterprising ex-naval officer.

At the top of the Pass the scenery is of the most

Cathedral Mountain.

rugged description, and the sensational character of the engineering increases as one commences the rapid descent towards the Columbia River.

Grand pines and thick undergrowth, rushing mountain torrents, and extensive vistas of peak and valley form an ever-varying and wild landscape.

The view of bleak and jagged crests overhead against the sky, and of steep pine-covered mountain slopes stretching out below, rocky and avalanche-swept, contrast with the bare expanses of river-channels on the broad valley-bottoms at their foot.

Grand, yet peaceful compared with the wild scenery of The Devil's Lake, is the view of the wide wooded valley of the great Columbia River as it bursts suddenly into view at Golden City, bounded on the west side by the snowy Selkirks, and on the east by the main range of the Rockies which we had just crossed.

The twin sources of the Columbia are fed by the snows of the Western slopes of the Rocky Mountains. The main river flows northward for nearly two hundred miles, makes a loop, known as the Big Bend, round the Selkirk range, and retraces its course southwards, flowing through Oregon to the Pacific.

Through its loop the Columbia drains both sides of the Selkirks, the two portions of the river being barely fifty miles apart. But only within the last three years was an accessible pass discovered over the range, and called the Rogers Pass after the explorer.

It is a region rich in minerals, timber, and game. Ten millions sterling worth of gold alone has been obtained by placer-mining from the beds of the rivers. The timber has been lavishly used in the construction of the railway. Mountain Creek, for example, is crossed by a trestle bridge 176 feet high and 600 feet long, while the bridge at Stoney Creek is believed to be the highest timber railway bridge in the world, being 296 feet in height and 450 feet in length.

The game is very shy, being much hunted by the Indians.

Leaving Golden City, where we camped for four days, the line passes Donald and follows alongside the river, whose curves form grand amphitheatres of rock rising thousands of feet overhead. The line soon enters Beaver Cañon, which it follows almost to the summit of the pass. Avalanches are numerous in winter, and to guard against them many miles of snow-sheds are being built. On both sides of the summit rise Mount Carrol (9560 feet) and Mount Hermit (8990), named from a rock near the latter which appears like a monk. The Selkirks as well as the Rockies proper are remarkable for the fantastic shapes of their summits. One forms a perfect pyramid, another resembles an old woman wearing a nightcap. The highest mountain of the Selkirk range is 11,000 feet, and lies south of the pass. It was named Syn-

Crossing the Selkirks; the Source of the Illecillewaet and the first Glacier near the summit of the Rogers Pass.

dicate Peak, but the Canadian Pacific Railway Company have named it Mount Sir Donald. The Illecillewaet River rises in a glacier near it, and flows westward from the summit of the pass into the Columbia. The railway as it descends follows along its banks. Close by at the mouth of the gorge from which it issues are the "loops" of the Canadian Pacific Railway, like the circular tunnels of the St. Gothard. Supported by large timber trestles, the line makes six loops and several curves one below the other, all in full view, and running for six miles, descends 600 feet, but advances meantime only two miles. Ille-cillewaet is an Indian word meaning "roaring torrent," and the stream is everywhere of that character, and flows in a deep and tortuous ravine. Douglas pines are now seen for the first time. Twenty miles from the Columbia lies the Albert Cañon, with a fall of 200 feet. As we approach the Columbia, Mount Begbie is seen towering over the river opposite to the settlement of Farwell, the name of which has lately been changed to Revelstoke. The Gold Range is the next to be passed.

Where can one see more original inscriptions than in a western town? "*Cleanliness is next to godliness, therefore go and wash at Johnson's bath-house on the river;*" or "*Nip and tuck shop;*" or "*Rooms to let,*" painted on a small battered tent; or a car with this notice—"*I am full of James' machines, hurry me along, farmers are waiting all along the line.*"

The line crosses the Columbia once more for the last time, and enters the Eagle Pass, 1996 feet above the Pacific. We had to pass the night at Farwell, and found our large amount of *impedimenta* a nuisance. Owing to the number of bad

characters prowling about during the construction of the line (many persons have lately been "held up" by them), we thought it right to sleep in the waggon with our baggage, and went on next day in a construction train filled with workmen to the top of the pass. Here we were transferred on to a "trolly," and then on to a "hand-car," which had to be built out with planks to give us standing room. The propelling gear was worked by Chinamen, numbers of whom are employed on the line, who seemed to find it hard work "pumping" us along.

How we crossed the Eagle Pass over the Gold Range on the Canadian Pacific Railway, British Columbia.

There are a few snow-capped peaks in the Gold Range, but they are lower than the Rockies and Selkirks, which seem as though just turned out from Vulcan's laboratory. The summits of the former appear to be more worn and rounded. In many places the forest fires have caused great devastation. Here and there notices are posted relative to the penalties incurred by those who are guilty of setting the wood on fire, but the origin of these fires is often most mysterious. The damper climate of the Pacific slopes will prevent the enormous damage which has occurred in many parts of the States.

At Griffin Lake there is fair trout-fishing. The settlers informed us that there are three kinds of fish. Reindeer were shot last winter on open park lands above, which are unseen as one passes through the valley below.

Crossing the Shuswap Lakes at Sikamous Narrows, we passed the night at the small hotel, the proprietor of which said he had campaigned with General Gordon in China. We had now reached a fine farming and ranching region comparatively well settled and populated, besides being a good hunting country, dry, hilly, and open.

It is as though a corner of the so-called great American Desert had been thrust into the south end of British Columbia, having its apex near Cariboo (the mail from which place has lately been "held up" and robbed).

This part is dotted with yellow pine; it can be traversed without trails, and forms the grazing ground of British Columbia.

The hired "cow-boys" on the ranches are mostly Shuswap Indians or Siwashes.

We took the steamboat, first up the Spellumacheen River, where we had a curious old "coloured person" with large spectacles as steward. His eyes, he said, "were tired of the world, and didn't want to see no more of it." Passing through peaceful agricultural scenery, we crossed the lakes to Kamloops at the junction of the North and South Thompson Rivers.

Yale—The Gateway to the Cañons of the Fraser.

Kamloops Lake is twenty miles in length.

It is here that the scenery of the Thompson River Cañon commences. Good trout-fishing can be had where the river leaves the lake. The Fraser and the Thompson River—the chief watercourses of British Columbia—meet at Lytton, and the stream now takes the name of the former.

Startling as was the ride through the Cañons of the Thompson, high above the wild torrent, across fissures and through cliffs, that through the Cañons of the Fraser River was still more striking. The rocky sides rise for thousands of feet like solid walls. The river runs at racehorse speed, while the railway is a succession of trestle bridges and tunnels, very costly to construct. The gorge ends at the small town of Yale.

The valley now widens out into flat forest and pasture land, with distant views of the coast ranges. We found the steamer at Port Hammond—a few hours from Victoria.

Vancouver is to be the terminus, 2900 miles west of Montreal, but it was burnt to the ground a couple of days ago, and will have to be rebuilt.

As the *Ancon* had just arrived from Portland, Oregon, there was no time for delay at Victoria, and I embarked alone the next day for Sitka, Alaska, *en route* for the Alpine regions lying south-east of Prince William Sound, and with the intention of at least seeing, if not of endeavouring to make the ascent of some of the Alps in the unexplored and unknown country of Mount St. Elias (20,000 feet), hitherto considered the highest mountain in North America. I found on board a party of two bound for the same spot, sent out by the *New York Times*, composed of Lieutenant F. Schwatka, late 9th U.S. Cavalry, and leader of the American Expedition to King William Land, and Professor W. Libbey of Princeton College. The island of Vancouver, named after George Vancouver, once a midshipman under Captain Cook, and afterwards the earliest explorer and surveyor of the coasts

Nanaimo.

of British Columbia from 30° N. latitude up to Russian territory, is 275 miles long and 85 miles broad, with mountains rising to 6000 feet. The settled portions and those fit for agriculture lie round Victoria and round Nanaimo Mines, the great coaling place.

Victoria was once, over thirty years ago, a post of the Hudson Bay Company, and grew into a settlement during the Fraser River gold "boom."

Indian Tiinkit Carvings on the Pacific Coast.

The railway from Victoria to Nanaimo will very soon be completed. Westward of Victoria lies the splendid harbour of Esquimault, used as a naval station by Her Majesty's ships. Victoria Harbour itself is small but excellent.

The seaward shores of Vancouver Island are very rocky and indented, and inhabited by a dissolute race of Indians. The Hydahs and the Timpseans were once great warriors, and use 80-foot canoes, carved out of a single Douglas fir-tree. Wild as the Vancouver Indians are, they are not by any means so depraved as are the uncivilised Queen Charlotte Islanders further north, living in islands almost entirely unexplored and unvisited. Many of the Vancouver Indians are employed in the Fraser River salmon-canneries, and are respectable sons of the Church.

The Chinese have invaded British Columbia with the same determination with which they have settled in California. Most of the domestic servants in Victoria are Chinamen.

As the last view one will have for a long time of the luxuries and ultra-comforts of civilisation, one gazes regretfully at the pretty villas with verandahs overgrown by creepers, and surrounded by gardens with luxuriant fruit and vegetables, in this semi-tropical climate. From March to November is a perpetual spring, while in winter the thermometer rarely falls below 40°.

Fair sport can be had on the northern and central parts of Vancouver Island in September and October with the wapiti, or American elk, and at any time during the season with the blacktail, or Virginian deer (*Cervus Columbianus*), which is found on all the islands northwards. In July and August the salmon will take a bait such as spoon-bait, notwithstanding all that has been said to the contrary, although they do not care for a fly. Trout can of course be caught with fly. On the mainland white mountain-goats can be found, and sometimes a few bears.

CHAPTER I.

Northwards from Victoria—The Great Sea-River, or the Inland Passage—Nanaimo—Tongass—Metlakatla—The Skeena River—Cape Fox—Loring—Wrangel—The Taku Inlet—Juneau—Chilcat and Chilcoot—Glacier Bay—Muir's Glacier—Sitka or New Archangel—A Fishing and Shooting Excursion—The Fourth of July at Sitka.

SITKA, ALASKA, *July 8th*, 1886.

THE province of British Columbia is no longer an unknown or uncared-for part of the British Empire. A new pathway, by the completion of the Canadian Railway, has brought her within a fortnight's journey of the mother country. Her gold and silver, her cattle and timber, fisheries and agriculture, and treasures of undeveloped wealth are teaching the nation that she is a land of giant future possibilities.

America's recent purchase, Alaska, will perhaps feel the benefit and will become a possession of increasing value.

The Pacific Coast Company's steamers make fortnightly trips during the summer up to Sitka by the inland passage. The least remarkable portions of the journey northwards are during the first five days. One is reminded of the tour usually made along the coasts of Norway. But the channels and armlets of British Columbia are narrower, more protected, dark, and intricate. The forests are quite unbroken, and the mountains higher and more continuous. Queen Charlotte Sound and part of Dixon Entrance are the only portions of the passage northwards not entirely protected from the heaviest swell from the Pacific Ocean or the strongest gales of wind. A more hilly, and at the same time a more densely wooded,

Stopping to Coal at Nanaimo, Vancouver's Island.

An Indian Totem Pole at Fort Wrangel.

country it would be hard to imagine, containing hardly one bare piece of flat ground, or ground of any kind not covered by spruce or cedar.

After leaving Victoria we stayed to coal at Nanaimo, having time to visit the mines by rail, and then steamed direct for Fort Tongass on American soil, just over the boundary line of Alaska, leaving all British posts, forts, mines, and fisheries for British vessels.

Opposite to Fort Tongass on the British side lies Fort Simpson, and near it Mr. Duncan's Indian Mission of Metlakatla, which boasts the organisation almost of a city, with Indian policemen and even a brass band.

Good wild mountain-goat hunting can be got from here by ascending the Skeena River, whither some English sportsmen have lately gone, returning in three weeks with eleven. Indeed the neighbourhood of Cape Fox is a great game country, principally for bears and goats. We next steamed across Dixon Entrance, where we had expected to feel the ocean swell, but were agreeably disappointed. So light are the summer nights in these high latitudes, that there is no stopping on the part of the steamer notwithstanding that there are no lighthouses, and that the channels are marvellously involved and intricate. To see what Nature can do in this respect one should glance on the chart at Kou Island, lying west of Fort Wrangel, to the shape of which the Coast Survey Commission could find no more appropriate resemblance than a mass of entrails thrown upon the ground. And it is an apt comparison.

After stopping for an hour at Loring, on the island of Revilla Gigedo, separated from the mainland by the narrow long channel called Behms Canal, we passed up the Duke of Clarence Straits in cloudy weather.

Fort Wrangel was our next point of call near the estuary of the Stikeen River, which was discolouring the sea for miles with muddy snow-water of a low temperature, the line of junction between the blue and the brown being very marked. A mail is carried from Fort Wrangel by canoe to the Mission on Prince of Wales Island at Howkan.

Fort Wrangel appears, in this wild wide land, as a comparatively large village. Indian carved Totem armorial poles can be seen and Indian curiosities and wares bought.

After quitting this settlement the narrow Wrangel Straits were passed by night and another cloudy

At Howkan.

morning which followed prevented our seeing some glaciers, the first which lie close to the route. But in the afternoon the mountains cleared as we steamed up Stephens Passage between Admiralty Island and the mainland. Some of the larger

Taku Inlet.

Southern Alaskan snow-fields and glaciers came into view for the first time as we passed the Taku Inlet with bold rocky *aiguilles* prominent at its head.

White mountain-goats can be found on the summits near here, but they are much hunted by the Indians.

The two young Frenchmen alluded to later on—Visconte de la R. and M. de la S.—afterwards went bear-hunting here. One writes to me as follows:—
"Nous avons fait a Taku Inlet un séjour très amusant et, malgré les conseils de B. et de tous les naturels du pays, j'ai chassé l'ours avec mon petit Winchester, ce qui ne m'a pas mal réussi, puisque j'en ai tué deux, dont un pesait 600 livres;

The Gold Mine on Douglas Island.

je crois qu'on nous a trouvés un peu fous dans le pays."

Close ahead we arrive at Harrisburg, *alias* Juneau City, a large mining settlement. On Douglas Island, immediately opposite, and facing the town, lies the largest mine in Alaska, the Paris or Treadwell quartz-mills, where gold literally flows like water. The gold-bearing ledge is like a quarry 500 feet in width. The ore is not rich, averaging from 9 to 50 dollars per ton; but the decomposed quartz is easily pulverised, and the supply inexhaustible. The amount of profit from the working of it is kept "dark," and is unknown; but it depends largely upon the employment of Chilcat Indians as labourers, who cost less than white men.

Three small creeks opposite lead to basins be-

Chilcat.

hind the mountains, where rich placer-mines have been worked for four seasons. The situation of Juneau is beautiful, but the mining population, together with the Indians camped there, form a rough "hard crowd" of both sexes—

> "Every prospect pleases,
> And man alone is vile."

Commercially the most valuable timber found in the neighbourhood is the red and yellow cedar, the latter said to be impervious to the *teredo* or boring worm; the white spruce is the common tree, growing to 175 feet in height and 6 feet in diameter.

Lynn's Canal is the long narrow arm that leads northwards till it divides at the head into the two

Eagle Glacier.

branch inlets of Chilcat (the pass over the mountains leading to the Yukon River), and Chilcoot. The Eagle Glacier is passed on the right, and Davidson's Glacier on the left, besides many others of smaller size.

As we rounded the curve of the inlet, the United States man-o'-war *Pinta* was seen lying at anchor.

It was half settled that, instead of hiring a schooner, as had been intended, I should join the *New York Times* Alaskan Expedition, which was the bearer of a recommendation from Secretary Whitney to the captain of the U.S.S. *Pinta*, to take the expedition two hundred miles north-west from Cape Spencer along the unprotected portion of coast as far as Yakatat Bay, at the foot of the St. Elias Alps.

Davidson Glacier.

Glacier Bay—so called from the number of glaciers which touch the sea, whither they descend from the southern verge of the frozen regions—is generally the next point of call. It is the best opportunity afforded for conveniently inspecting an Alaskan glacier.

In front of Muir's Glacier, on the eastern shores, the water is deep up to the very edge of the ice, which rises like a broken wall, and from which a shower of icebergs of varied size is constantly falling into the ocean which laves its foot and undermines its green and glassy fissures.

This glacier has recently been investigated by an American scientist. Glacier Bay is thirty miles long and eight to twelve miles wide. At the mouth is a cluster of thirty islands named Beardslee, composed of glacial *débris*. The width of the ice where the glacier breaks through the mountains is 10,664 feet, and of the water-front one mile, being as much as 400 feet high in places. Nine large and seventeen smaller branches unite to form the main ice-stream. From measurements and observations, it appears that a stream of solid ice 5000 feet wide, and 700 feet deep, is entering the sea at a rate of forty feet per day, in the month of August.

Not a tree can be seen (and it is almost a relief after the endless forests of the archipelago) upon the steep, ice-worn, smooth rocky hills of Glacier Bay.

In a westerly direction across the inlet, under the red rays of the setting sun, Mounts Crillon (15,900 feet), Fairweather (15,500 feet), and La Pérouse appear in dim outline as the mighty *vedettes* of that vast icy Switzerland beyond and partly bordering the sea, of the presence of which we are aware, although most of its characteristics are unknown.

When we woke next morning we were passing through Peril Straits where the *Eureka* foundered in the "tide rip" in the narrowest part upon a rock.

Sitka is prettily situated in a sound about thirty miles across, and bordered with mountains from

Sitka and Mount Edgcumbe.

four to six thousand feet high, covered most of the year with snow. Years since, it was the headquarters of the Russian Trading Company, whose ponderous wood buildings are still the largest in the settlement.

The extinct volcano of Mount Edgcumbe lies across the bay, with vertical stripes of snow on its sides. Our party made it 1022 metres in height. At the arrival of each steamer the inhabitants of

Sitka agree to go mad. Indian maidens dance with miners, and night, never very dark, is turned into day. Meanwhile the squaws drive a good trade in articles of native manufacture and even in such things as young bear and blacktail deer.

At Juneau City. A young bear for five dollars.

The *Pinta* had to wait a fortnight before she could take us north, for coals and for the mails. It was therefore decided that we should make a fishing and hunting excursion, which the Sitka paper (for a weekly journal is published) described as "a party of young gentlemen in search of the picturesque in Nature and the exciting in adventure. They are procuring Indian guides and evidently mean business, though it is all for pleasure."

We hired three Indians and a large war-canoe, with a smaller one for fishing.

A full-sized hydah or war-canoe measures some

thirty feet in length, and can sail ten knots with a good breeze. We first camped some miles away from Sitka by some old Russian weirs, where every moment a salmon or a salmon trout might be seen darting, as one gazed, out of the briny foam into the fresh water of the lake hard by, from which it is divided by some rocky channels only a few yards in length, some of which are natural and others artificial, these latter dating from the Russian occupation.

A solitary white man in charge directs the operations of salting the salmon-bellies; while each morning the hired Indians arrived from some spot in the bay known only to themselves with a large canoe-load of "silver" salmon.

He "means business, though it is all for pleasure."

Large quantities of salmon refuse are thrown into the sea, where numbers of enormous cat-fish and dog-fish can be seen struggling for the morsels, giving us good sport with a salmon rod and line baited with a lump of fish, fighting as they did when once hooked madly for their liberty. Some salmon were caught with a spoon-bait before leaving for Mount Edgcumbe, where plenty of deer are to be found. During the next few days it rained and blew, but when camp is pitched by the shore just within the forest the enormous firs give excellent protection; the only discomfort exists in the richness of the verdant undergrowth, the normal and constant con-

dition of which is one of dampness. Forest fires are unknown on these islands. This dampness covers the fallen trees and the whole surface of the ground with a deep soft moss, and renders the forest scene one of tropical beauty and luxuriance. The only successful method of shooting the deer on the islands is the one we employed during the short time we remained on Kruzoff Island, on which the above volcano is situated.

After a ten mile tramp of the most fatiguing kind we reached the slopes of Edgcumbe, and ascended to the higher ground where they feed. Every one being carefully hidden, the Indians brought the deer within range by imitating the cry of the fawns by blowing on a blade of grass. Each of us killed one within an hour, but it is an unsatisfactory sort of sport from its very certainty of success.

We found ourselves back at Sitka once more, in

The Final Heat.

time for the 4th of July celebrations, including an "oration" by the judge, a baseball match, Indian canoe races, and one of the "balls" for which that hospitable place is famous. And while our rooms are in Governor Swineford's house, Ah Sow's small restaurant furnishes us with meals. Eventually the *Idaho* has arrived with coal, passengers, and mails. The two bright boys from Chicago have

The Judge practises the Chinook Language—"Siwash sik tum-tum o-cook kum tux."

shipped their Indians and war-canoe for Glacier Bay after bears; while my French friends M. de la S. and Visconte de la R. have embarked for the Taku Inlet. Our time at Sitka is drawing to a close.

CHAPTER II.

From Sitka to the Alaskan Alps—The U.S.S. *Pinta*—Mount Fairweather—Arrival at Yakatat—The Mount St. Elias range—The Yakatat Indians—The Swedish Traders—Indian Curiosities—The Man-o'-War at the Village—Interviews with the Chief.

ABOARD THE U.S. MAN-O'-WAR *Pinta*,
YAKATAT BAY, ALASKA, *July* 14*th*, 1886.

ON the morning of July 10th, the *New York Times* Expedition to Mount St. Elias and Icy Bay embarked on a small whaleboat lying alongside the wharf at Sitka. The members of the expedition had just had their photographs taken, and their provisions, tents, and instruments were on the maindeck of the U.S.S. *Pinta*. Was it not an auspicious commencement? For this also was the name of the vessel which bore Columbus to the new world, and we too were bound to the westward intent on new discoveries.

The *Alaskan*, published at Sitka, favoured us with the following paragraph :— " Lieutenant Schwatka's party for a two month's siege of the ice-guarded fortress of Mount St. Elias is now made up and ready for the march. The party consists, besides the Lieutenant, of Professor W. Libby and Mr. H. W. Seton Karr. Also Joseph Woods, John Dalton, and Kersnuk, an Indian youth."

The *Pinta* (Commander Nicholls, U.S.N.) was built, we were told, originally as a tug-boat, and as her speed did not exceed four to five knots an hour, she was an easy object for an " instantaneous shutter" as she steamed past the old Russian wharf. But the *Pinta* is well suited for cruising in the calm *fiords* of the inland passage, or for punishing refractory Indians, or Tlinkits as they are called on this part of the coast, by destroying their villages with her machine guns and brass howitzers, and for lying at anchor off the small but gay old Russian village of Sitka, or the new and unpleasant, though picturesquely situated, mining-village before-mentioned of Juneau City, or Harrisburg,—for it enjoys a double name.

It was said at one time that other vessels on sighting her were in the habit of flying signals of distress, because, owing to some eccentricity in her rudder, and the fact that she had run down several other vessels, they were fearful of suffering the same fate themselves.

Several channels may be used to reach the open sea from Sitka. We might either have gone out at once across Sitka Sound, or have kept entirely to the inland passage—a longer route—as far as Cross Sound. A middle course was chosen which gave us a few hours along one of the calm Alaskan channels before meeting the ocean swell.

Sunset found us skirting the steep shores of

Mount Fairweather, rising to 15,500 feet above the North Pacific Ocean at its base.

Chichagoff Island in lat. 57° 50', the weather continuing beautifully fine.

Mount Fairweather consented to show itself for only a short time next morning, but in the afternoon, as we steamed slowly past, about twenty miles from land, the whole Fairweather range was seen in a cloudless atmosphere, and remained in view till sunset, when the darkness, and the necessity of early rising on the morrow, drove us below.

The next morning, July 12th, as I came on deck at an early hour we were rounding Ocean Cape and heading for the small harbour near the Indian village, charted by the U.S. Coast Survey, and named Port Mulgrave. It was the *Pinta's* second visit. There was no trace of vapour in the sky. The St. Elias range of Alps, or a great portion of them, bound the west side of this bay, which is called Yakatat or Bering Bay.

Without a doubt the scenery at Yakatat is the most wonderful of its kind in the whole world. The mountains are covered with snow and glaciers from sea-level to summit. The air of early morning in latitude 60° N. is exceedingly transparent, while the vastness of these mountains, ranging as they do from 16,000 to nearly if not quite 20,000 feet, impress the beholder under these conditions with the sensation of their being too ethereal to have any actual existence, or that they cannot be anything except some unholy illusion that must dissolve and disperse when the sun rises. And this is to a certain extent what happens. It seemed to be just what Doré might have conceived as an imaginary view of mountain scenery in the planet Mars.

As the sun rose higher, the shadows grew less distinct, the planes of distance merged into each other, the air lost its extreme brilliancy, and the exact contours became confused. Yet we could hardly believe that the great mass of Mount St. Elias, the pointed crest of which rose high above the sea, was between fifty and sixty miles off.

Imagine Mont Blanc placed close to the sea-shore with its whole height visible as measured from the sea-level; then imagine Ben Nevis, the highest mountain in Great Britain, placed upon the summit of Mont Blanc, and the total height thus reached would fall short of the summit of Mount St. Elias. The latest estimate of its height by the Coast Survey has made it nearly 20,000 feet, with an error either way of a few hundred feet.

St. Elias—the last and highest mountain of the range, and the nearest to the sea—stands on a broad base, from which it rises like an Egyptian pyramid, straight, regular, and massive, from an icy plateau of enormously extensive glaciers.

Could a blind man be brought to Yakatat, and have his sight restored while each morsel of the panorama, commencing from the east, was separately presented to his view, he would exclaim at first that nothing could surpass its grandeur in that direction; then, as his gaze would gradually be shifted round to the west, still loftier mountain-ranges would disclose themselves, till he would think he must surely have arrived at the climax.

Higher and higher yet they would rise as Mounts Cook and Vancouver were passed in review, while words would fail him to express his astonishment as last of all his eyes would rest on Mount St. Elias, the crown and summit of all possibilities or impossibilities of grandeur, seeming to rise sheer out of the Pacific Ocean with a leap.

From Elias eastward, a semicircle of enormous peaks surrounds the Bay, gradually dwindling in importance and in height, even the smallest of them being a noble mountain; while far back towards the east, from which we had come, Mount Fairweather, which is 16,000 feet in height, glistened with opalescent light above the forest trees.

Entering the small land-locked harbour at six A.M. by the narrow entrance,—with which Captain Nicholls was already acquainted, having been in command of the *Pinta* last year when she visited this place, we dropped anchor close to the Indian village.

Not a living thing was visible except a dejected wolfish-looking dog. The natives were evidently out sealing, and we might be delayed in our start for Icy Bay.

However, after blowing a whistle for some time, canoes were seen coming from some houses on the mainland. The first contained an old half-blind Yakatat Indian of characteristic appearance, who was evidently a "shawaan" or medicine-man by his long uncut hair. By means of a half-breed boy employed in the ward-room, who spoke better English than our interpreter, he was made to

Mount Vancouver, 13,100 feet.

understand that we wished him to despatch a messenger to the tribe to procure for us two large canoes and six Indians. He set off on his errand with a great appearance of haste, after explaining that it would take two days, being a long journey towards the head of the Bay where the tribe was sealing. Nothing was left but to wait, and as Captain Nicholls had determined to see us fairly started and on the road, the *Pinta* waited too.

Meanwhile, we were able to take the bearings of Mounts Cook, Vancouver, and Malaspina, besides other nameless peaks. The wild strawberries were now ripe and grew in great abundance on the sand-hills round the village, while the "snipe" which congregated in flocks along the edge of the sea were found to be excellent eating, especially with clam sauce. In the absence of their owners the Indian houses were locked up, but I was able to make a sketch of St. Elias. Before long, to our surprise, two white men made their appearance alongside in a "dory" or small boat, and turned out to be two young Swedes newly arrived as traders to replace the famous Dr. Ballou. One of them, whose name was Louis Carlsen, informed us that he had come to Alaska four years ago from Stromsdal near Gothenburg, and that with his brother and two other Swedes by the name of Andersen they had taken up the "store" built here two years ago by the Alaska Commercial Company and vacated last year as not profitable, as well as a small store which they had constructed on Kaiak Island further up the coast, where they were engaged in hunting and in trading with the natives.

He further informed us that his partners would call here next month, in a small schooner they owned; following the example of one of them, he intended to visit his home in Sweden, and return from thence in the spring, with a wife. He expressed himself as very pleased to see the man-o'-war, because the Indians had lately become troublesome and threatening, but now they would do whatever was required of them. He had even been obliged to menace them with the visit of a

The Village of the Yakatat Indians.

man-o'-war if they did not behave. Our timely arrival had thus acted as a corroboration of his threat. The Yakatats have lately been distilling a good deal of the vile spirit like *vodki* from sugar, and have been so frequently drunk that the traders were glad their store was as far removed from the village as it was. His brother Olaf was waiting for him at Kaiak Island and would return with him to Sweden, for the first and last time in twelve years. Their small schooner would be laid up to winter at Kaiak. From thence they would go by canoe to Prince William Sound, where they could pick up the Alaska Commercial Company's schooner, and thus reach Kodiak Island, where probably a vessel would call in September, on her way to San Francisco, from Unalaska, or if not, the schooner itself would be going down to California.

It was not, altogether, with unmixed pleasure we found that there were white traders here, as we had been informed that the post had not been taken up since the Alaska Commercial Company had vacated it, and that the natives did not now make use of, or understand money as a medium of exchange. We had, in consequence, brought a supply of "trading material" with us. We managed, however, to get rid of it, and it made no difference in the end, except entailing a terrible amount of haggling, "chin-music" as the lieutenant styled it, with the Yakatat Indians.

Next morning "George," the second chief, came on board, and was followed soon after by Noearpoo, the chief of the Yakatats, dressed in a U.S.S. *Adams* riband and uniform, presented to him when that vessel came to arrest and bring to justice the murderer of two white men. It appears that the latter had come to "prospect" for indications of gold, and that soon after their arrival the Indian or Indians, for some fancied grudge, had shot down both of them as they were landing from their boat.

All the visits of white men to Yakatat, few and far between, seem to have been attended with misfortune, for another party which also landed from a man-o'-war, with the object of exploring the source of some gold-containing black sand,* became so much discouraged by the accidental deaths from drowning of some members of the party soon after their arrival, that they gave up their investigations and returned to Sitka without accomplishing their object.

Meanwhile the chief, with his gorgeous coloured neckcloth and gold uniform, had been taken to the captain's cabin, where, with the two interpreters, we descended to interview him. After a long speech, which he had evidently prepared beforehand, about white men always speaking the truth and Indians sometimes, he was asked for information, and told us that some of the Indians were in the habit of

* This was subsequently visited and inspected by our party while awaiting the return of the gunboat.

hunting in the neighbourhood of Icy Bay, but "when they tried to come near the great mountain, then Indians always died," as the interpreter rendered it, meaning they failed; also that Icy Bay * was " best place, for Indians no cross ice."

After more talk the captain presented him with a U.S.S. *Pinta* riband to wear instead of the *Adams* one, and the interview was over. Meantime, another canoe was despatched up the Bay to fetch a man said to have been half-way up Mount St. Elias. I strongly suspected these were merely pretexts to keep us here as long as possible, since it was evident to them that the ship was on a peaceful errand. For it afterwards appeared, according to the assertion of the chief, who was jealous of "George," the man despatched in the canoe, that the latter did not start until the next day.

It was also more than probable that Mr. Nocarpoo had never been very far away, but on the sight of the war-vessel had hastily " vacated the situation " and left for " parts unknown," until satisfied that she had not come to bombard his village. But it was

* The Great Agassiz Glacier or the Malaspina Plateau might preferably be crossed by future expeditions, the landing being made at Yakatat Bay instead of Icy Bay, in order to avoid the surf at the latter place.

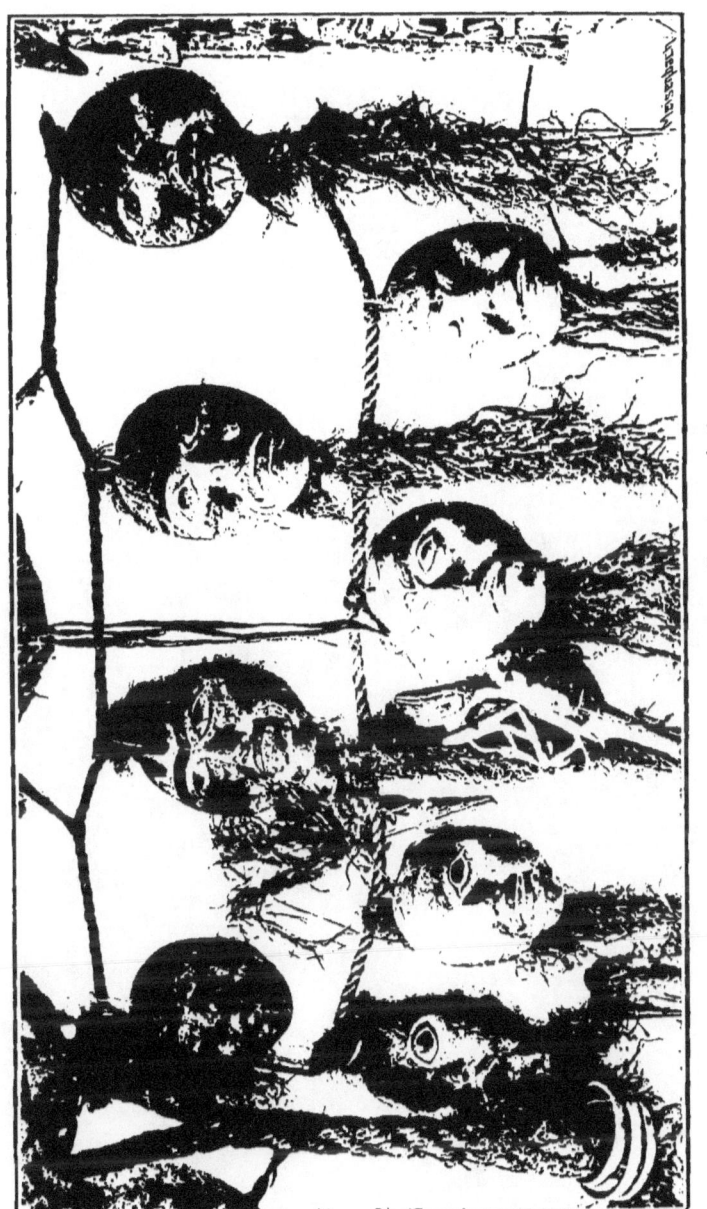

Spirit-Masks from the Yakatat Indian Sorcerer's Grave.

natural enough that the Indians should have been anxious to prolong the stay of the vessel, for money soon began to be in brisk circulation. Many curios were brought to the ship's side and at once bought up by the officers who were making collections of native objects. The Indians too were now all the more desirous of money, as a disreputable Indian woman, known as Mrs. Toms, had made her way up from Sitka in a large hydah or war-canoe, and was busy trading, and supposed to be possessed of a large fortune amassed by doubtful methods. The greater part of the articles of native manufacture brought for sale consisted in baskets of a variety of shapes, neatly plaited out of roots, dyed different colours and designed in different patterns; charms, carved walrus tusks, bows and arrows, and horn spoons. Some one went out in a canoe and made a great "find" of some boxes in the grave of a medicine-man in a retired part of the bay. Whenever a "shawaan" dies his charms and other articles that he has used are placed in boxes, buried with him, and left to rot unless rescued as curios, for no Indian will touch them. As no Indian even dares to approach the grave of a medicine-man, the abstractions can never be discovered or lamented. In the evening the two sacksfull were spread out on the floor in the captain's cabin for inspection, and comprised, among other things, a quantity of masks of painted wood, a leather shawl, ornamented with sea-parrots' bills, and a crown of wild-goats' horns. Some one else had bought for a few cents a charm hung on a string and resembling a small whetstone. The use of this for a long time rested a mystery until our Tlinkit interpreter discovered that, during three days previous to starting out sealing, the Yakatat Indians are not to scratch their backs with the hand, but when the irritation becomes absolutely unendurable they may use such stones as these like scrapers. Any man violating this rule will probably be drowned—accidentally.

Everything not to be taken with us to Icy Bay was stored in the chief's house. I found that my large Alpine hat had been left at Sitka, and therefore had another one made by the quartermaster out of sail-cloth. It was light and comfortable; the brim was of enormous size, and was the subject of much pleasantry, such as, "When the top of Elias is seen to assume an umbrella shape, then we shall know for certain that the party has attained that much-desired spot." To make sure of having a comfortable hat, another one, of basket-work, was ordered from the chief's wife, who promised to put it in hand at once; but not even the assurance that "the Queen of England would see it" was sufficient to ensure its being more than an unfulfilled promise.

CHAPTER III.

We leave Yakatat for Icy Bay—Landing in the Surf—The Base Camp—Strawberries and Bear-Trails—The Start for Mount St. Elias—Fording a Glacial Torrent—A Mighty Stream—The Quicksands—A Mountainous Moraine Overgrown with Forest—An Ice-buried River.

CAMP BY THE SEASHORE,
ICY BAY, *July* 18*th*, 1886.

AFTER our one brilliant day it rained continuously the remainder of the time the *Pinta* was at Yakatat, a period altogether of five days, during which the natives found other pretexts for delaying us. A man was sent to ask leave to use a large canoe said to be laid by in a lagoon—two days' journey, for the owner was out sealing. He returned, and the men were to have set off to fetch the canoe at three o'clock next morning, in order to catch high-tide, but did not actually start until mid-day, and then came back with the intelligence that she was decayed and rotten.

Then the United States Navy, in the shape of Captain Nicholls, came to the rescue. He would take us to Icy Bay in the *Pinta*, and we were to be allowed to use one of the whale-boats until we were fetched away, or came down to Sitka in the fall of the year. If possible, the *Pinta* would return for us about the 5th of September.

On the evening of July 16th, at eight o'clock, the *Pinta* steamed out of Yakatat, having shipped three Indians and a small "dug-out" Yakatat canoe, the property of Professor Libbey, large enough to hold two persons comfortably.

After the Fourth of July Oration by "the Judge," which we had been favoured with at Sitka, in which he read the "Declaration of Independence" and protested against the crimes of "the old country," and which I had endeavoured, however, to applaud, it was considered to be a matter of surprise that I should have plucked up sufficient spirit to suggest that Mount St. Elias might be entirely, and must be one fourth, in British territory.*

* Mount St. Elias, hitherto considered the highest mountain in North America (though now, according to Lieutenant Allen, Mount Wrangel, a volcano at the forks of the Copper River, in Eastern Central Alaska, rises to over 20,000 feet), is the longest snow-climb in the world outside the Arctic or Antarctic regions, and with the additional exception of Greenland, is the birthplace of the most extensive glaciers known. Of these, there are probably 2400 square miles of FLAT plains of ice between the mountains and the sea, not taking into account snow-fields or inland glaciers, and included

The boundary line between British Columbia and South-East Alaska, according to the treaty, cannot be at a greater distance from the ocean than thirty miles. But if the divide or summit of the watershed be less than that distance from the sea, then the boundary follows the summit of the watershed up to the 141st degree of longitude. It then runs due north, coinciding with the 141st meridian, until it joins the Arctic Ocean.

At four o'clock next morning we were slowly coasting along the shores of Icy Bay in a dense foggy rain. Nothing could be imagined more dismal. We were cheered by the thought that we must be considerably closer to Mount St. Elias than we were at Yakatat, and indeed we were prepared to see it towering overhead through some break in the clouds, if they only would break. But the *Pinta's* last view of Mount St. Elias was that from Yakatat, for not until after her departure

entirely between Cross Sound, at the extremity of the Inland Passage, and the Copper River. Vancouver, who had, as he says, many opportunities for fixing the true position of the great mountain, gives it as lat. 60° 27', and long. 140° 39'. Professor Davidson gives its position as lat. 60° 22' 6", and long. 140° 54'. It thus lies to the east of the 141st meridian of longitude west from Greenwich, confirmed by my own bearings, the range itself ranking as the third highest in the world, on which we had set foot for the first time.

did the range break loose from its encircling clouds.

Probably this was the first time that a ship has ever entered Icy Bay, by which name the slight angle in the coast-line is honoured, so caution was necessary. The growing day disclosed a sandy sloping shore, without the least indication of shelter from the ocean, stretching away straight, remorseless, and yellow on either side as far as the eye could reach east and west, white with roaring breakers, and half obscured by fog. As the Indians asserted they were in the habit of running their canoes ashore here when they came sealing, the ship was brought to an anchor.

The Pacific swell rolled slowly under us towards the beach, on which it was breaking with a threatening aspect very disturbing to landsmen. Clouds of spray and vapour drifted inland, but behind the beach there seemed to lie lagoons which were steaming, as though warm, and further off still there were visible the tops of fir-trees. Then the mist closed down and everything was hidden.

The Pacific surf is very uncertain, and rises or calms down without apparent cause, as the result of distant storms at sea. Still, on this part of the Alaskan shore-line, Fairweather Ground, as the whalers named it, fine weather is generally experienced in summer, with calms, which are not agreeable to sailing vessels. But how the winds blow in winter!

Shortly after we had dropped anchor, Lieutenant Dumbough was sent in one of the waistboats to examine the surf, and at midday Lieutenant-Commander Nicholls determined to do his best to put us ashore with the supplies. Lieutenant Emmons, in charge of the first boat, put off at once from the ship's side, and after waiting his opportunity was able to beach his boat stern first, paying out an anchor rope from the bows, the anchor having been dropped fifty yards from shore to assist in putting off again through the breakers.

As soon as she grounded the sailors jumped into the water and ran her up high and dry. At times as seen from the ship the little boat had appeared quite submerged behind some big roller.

Four boatloads sufficed to land the whole of the stores of supplies and instruments. Although the boats were empty on their return, yet the task of launching them again through the surf was one of more danger than the landing.* The last boat

* I think if the surf had been any higher we should have been

beached being the one that was to remain with us in default of our having obtained hydah-canoes at Yakatat, had no anchor laid out for launching, and was securely hauled up out of reach of the tide on the crest of the sand ridge.

Perhaps the best part of the day's performance was that of "Bear Hunter," our best Yakatat, who died a few days after from poison, and who volunteered to steer the little canoe, hewn out a single small tree, without any assistance, through the surf, being carried eventually on the crest of a wave high upon the beach, where we were all waiting to receive him.

The little party of five whites and four Indians, "the first that ever burst" on to the wild shores of Icy Bay, was now fairly on the way. The *Pinta* had succeeded in putting us ashore in a very wet condition (but not nearly so wet as we were to be when we tried to depart). As she steamed southwards she whistled a farewell note, but our cheers in reply must have been drowned by the noisy surf.

The camp was pitched by the freshwater lagoon which we had seen behind the ridge. The ground

unable to land. Future explorers, if any further attempts are made to ascend Mount St. Elias, should land either at Cape Yagtag or Yakatat Bay.

was covered and almost hidden in places by ripe strawberries of fabulous size, and was crossed in various directions by bear-tracks, also of a fabulous size as it seemed. As soon as everything had been stowed and the tents pitched, the Indians went sealing. Seal meat and blubber are as necessary to the Indian as bread to the white man. They soon returned with a seal and a wild swan, plenty of which birds were flying round the lagoon uttering harsh cries, their white plumage contrasting strongly against the dark woods behind, which in turn contrasted with the ice beyond them. It was fullsized, but had not been able to fly, for the feathers were immature. Later on I pursued one of these birds successfully in the canoe, which nearly got capsized during the operation from the recoil of the gun.

Some of the bear-tracks along the beach, close to the camp, measured fourteen inches by eight, and there are many others no doubt much larger. Bear and fox trails cross the sandy soil in every direction like a network, giving one the idea that enormous numbers of these animals must inhabit the very small piece of forest on this side of the bay, which is the only piece in the whole region, for everything else seems to be snow and glacier.

To-day being Sunday we remain quietly at rest, and start early to-morrow for "the great mountain," as the Indians call it. At rest, that is, with the exception of the preparations for a fortnight's assault on the mountain, testing the mercurial barometers and the thermometers, and making the arrangements involved in a scientific and mountaineering expedition. Dalton, who is cook, is to stay in charge of everything here, which will be a sort of base of operations. However, Woods, who goes with us, cooks nearly as well. We take fifty pounds of "hard tack," twenty-five pounds of flour, ten pounds of chocolate, besides tea, sugar, coffee, and various tins of canned meat; in fact, enough for nearly two weeks with the additional supplies when the Indians return for them. Also three magazine rifles, all of the same calibre. Among the scientific apparatus, mostly the property of the Professor, come two large mercurial mountain barometers, a hypsometer, and several aneroids and thermometers. A prismatic compass lent to me by the Royal Geographical Society, will be one of the most useful of all our instruments. We take also two small tents from Edgington's (London), which will prove exceedingly useful, the two tents presented by the Northern Pacific Railway to the expedition being too large for packing. Amongst other things are two alpenstocks and two ice-axes, fashioned after a rude manner by a Russian blacksmith at Sitka; besides one real English ice-axe, which I found being used as a hoe by an old Russian peasant, who had no conception of its original use; waterproofs and blankets for the party, and for my own use a sleeping bag made out of opossum skin, while the Indians seem to be satisfied with a cotton sheet only as night covering. The Professor contributes half-a-dozen pairs of "ice-creepers" as used at Niagara Falls, in which he places greater confidence than in the ice-axes. We have also some Esquimaux clothing for use on the ice, the property of Mr. Schwatka, and for the ascent a coil of two hundred feet of rope.

After the arrangements for to-morrow were nearly completed, I went out with our "prospector" to look for bears, but as Elias gave signs of becoming visible, and the bears did not, I hurried back to camp to make some sketches. After a time the mountain slowly appeared like a dissolving view, while the summit played hide-and-seek with the clouds, which were shifting uneasily like side-scenes at a pantomime, preparatory to a general movement. The Indians went out in the evening, and came back with more seals and a red fox. A seal meanwhile came up on the beach close to camp. Over fifteen hundred hair-seals are said to have been killed in three days, by a party in Yakatat Bay, with clubs, and considering the large numbers we have seen, and the ease with which the Indians seem to go out and club them, it is not difficult to believe it.

The Indians hunt the seals systematically in Yakatat Bay, where they are consequently very shy. We saw large numbers in the sea on our return, but besides being contrary to the laws of the United States, it would be useless for any party of white men to hope to kill more than one or two.

One can pass the time very comfortably among the sand-hills, which are perfect natural strawberry beds, moving a few yards further to fresh ground as the supply on the spot becomes exhausted; meantime keeping a look-out along the edge of the forest, over the long grass, for the grey-coloured round back of a St. Elias cinnamon or grizzly bear. These animals evidently come out in large numbers after seal (or strawberries), judging by the immense quantity of tracks.

The trails are thickest at that point on the beach where the forest approaches nearest to the sea, for the great brown bear of Alaska is a shy animal, and when he comes out in the afternoon about four o'clock, his favourite hour, to catch a seal, he likes to have his retreat handy.

A mile or two away wide stretches of water can be seen through openings in the forest, evidently the large lake which the early navigators saw from the mastheads of their ships, and which is marked in their maps as being of considerable extent. Our Indians say plenty of fish can be got there.

The side of Icy Bay, on which we are now camped, is low, flat forest, some ten miles either way, and bounded on the land side by the enormous glaciers which are just visible over the fir-trees. The west side of Icy Bay, as can be seen, is formed by a glacier which has projected itself for some distance into the ocean.

The Second Camp, July 20th,
Sunset.

Yesterday we left the base camp at seven in the morning. The Professor was left behind in order to effect simultaneous observations with the second mercurial barometer, and will rejoin us to-morrow with the Indians, who have returned for more supplies.

After transporting the things in the small canoe for half a mile up the lagoon, which then came to a sudden end, the packs were adjusted, and the party followed the shore to the westward, more or less under the guidance of the Indians, who were making for the large river at the head of the Bay, intending that we should follow up the bank.

The Start for Mount St. Elias.

Woods carried a tent, spade, pick, and pan, for gold-prospecting purposes. Schwatka carried the mercurial barometer and a rifle. I carried the ice-axes and another rifle; the remaining things were divided equally into packs among the Indians of about fifty or sixty pounds to each pack.

After following the shore for two miles an offshoot of the main glacial river was reached, over which the Indians conveyed us on their backs, although the greatest depth was but three feet. The heaviest of us, who weighed eighteen stone, was landed quite dry upon the opposite bank, while the lightest of the three was deposited halfway over in a sitting position in a foot and a half of water; such are the uncertainties of fate!

This stream issued from the forest across flats of glacier mud, and came from the direction in which we were going as a shallow muddy stream. We wished to follow it up, but the Indians, probably on account of what they had been told at Yakatat, were disinclined to do so. It would have been better had we done so, for it was, as we suspected, an offshoot from the main river at the head of Icy Bay, and would have saved a long *détour*. Had we then known of the miles of ice-cold water we should have to wade through yesterday, of the deep creeks, and of the mud and quicksands to be passed, and how wet and chilled the party was to be before night, we should have disdained being carried across this stream by the Indians.

After this came a fine wide sandy plain lying between the belt of timber and the ocean, covered with sweet-smelling tall purple flowers, rushes, and wild strawberries in profusion, and dotted with small fir-trees growing more thickly towards the forest, and more sparsely scattered towards the ocean. Three miles further and our progress to the west was barred by the main stream, up the left bank of which the way now lay.

We were on the edge of the forest and on the bank of a large glacial river which was spread out in the shape of a fan, and appeared to issue from between a glacier and a line of elevated land. It was a large river, but not larger than one might expect, as forming one of the many streams which drain the vast expanse of snow and ice which covers and encircles the St. Elias range. Schwatka at once named it "Jones' River," after the proprietor of the *New York Times*. Its main stream appeared to issue from the apex of its fan-shaped delta, but many smaller ones joined it, rushing out from under the ice of the opposite glacier, which we named the "Guyot Glacier," after that distinguished scientist. We had been aware that a glacier existed there, for it forms the west side of Icy Bay, and has been named Icy Cape, and described by numerous navigators, from Vancouver and Beechey to Tebenkoff and the United States Coast Survey.

Across a gravelly delta six miles wide, edged in on the opposite shore by a glacier, the river lay spread in numberless channels, shallow, swift, ice-cold, and milk-white with a brownish tinge, and a black oily scum. It reached and swept back the ocean across a long bar marked out by angry lines of surf. Bears had recently been travelling along the margin, and had left fresh tracks. After stopping to sketch and rest, we followed northwards up the bank of the river. The Indians went slowly, and lagged behind. The day had turned out cloudless and the sun was hot. Wide expanses of mud were crossed. The surface was firm, tenacious, shaking, and jelly-like—a crust, as it seemed, floating on soft and treacherous quicksands. On one of these mud-flats an especially soft place had to be crossed, and the dread of a possible breaking through the crust made it nervous work. Woods got over first and crossed a channel on to firm ground; the Indians following dropped part of their packs to lighten themselves, sinking thigh deep as they did so. In their tracks lanes of water were left on the surface of the mud, as though squeezed from a sponge. This part seemed firmer as we followed. Whether this was the case, or our broad-soled boots saved us, we sank in less than was to be expected.

The party rested, considerably exhausted, for

an hour on the other side, on *terra firma*, and continued the march at 2 P.M., along a wooded point which stretched far out into the wide bed of the main river, and crossing a side stream by means of a fallen tree, arrived at more mud-flats, but kept this time near the grass and rushes, which grew along the edge of the forest. It might be supposed that the forest was preferable to rivers and quicksands; but the growth was so dense as to offer but very slow prospects of locomotion to men with packs on their backs. The river, like all rivers of glacial source, was now on the usual daily rise, and had invaded the flat lands, while the water felt icy cold to the feet, which were numbed and senseless after such prolonged wading. Bruin is the great road-maker of Alaska, and we had been following mostly in his broad beaten tracks.

About 5 P.M. further progress directly north towards Mount St. Elias became barred by a huge buried glacier, overtopped by immense masses of moraine and overgrown thickly with shrubs and fir-trees, which were becoming disordered and destroyed where they grew on the edges or faces of the moraines by reason of the slow but irresistible movement forward of the mass urged on by the pressure of the glaciers behind. This had appeared from the base-camp as a low range of hills. We now saw its true nature. It was the face of a glacier, buried by immense masses of terminal moraine, which, being overgrown with trees, had seemed from a distance like ordinary hilly ground. Now and then avalanches of stones rattled down its slopes. Ice protruded in places. Torrents burst up through the stones like rivers, created full-grown without any infancy or childhood, issuing from some mountain side. One particularly large one we named Fee Springs. Climbing some distance up to reconnoitre, it was seen that a mile further on the timber grew gradually thinner, and gave place to gravel; we decided to camp there on a dry part of the river bed.

The flat expanse of the estuary lay stretched seawards, fringed by the black line of timber which we had skirted, and bounded by a vast glacier named afterwards the "Great Guyot Glacier," having its face so bespattered with rocks and dirt that only here and there was the ice visible. This glacier seemed to extend from this point quite flat for ten or fifteen miles westward, and at least twenty miles south-west by south far out into the sea, thus forming the west side of Icy Bay, named by previous explorers Icy Cape. On climbing up the moraine after bears yesterday evening I found progression so difficult that a return to camp was preferable to destroying one's clothes on the chance of a shot.

For supper we had chocolate, bacon, and "hard-tack." One of the Indians slept wrapped in a sheet on the gravel, with his head on a coil of rope; the others made a tent out of withes and a ground-sheet. Woods and Kersunk, or Fred, as he prefers to be called, put up one of the tents. Schwatka and myself should have done the same, as the mosquitoes were troublesome, but we slept in the open.

This morning at 9 A.M. the Indians started back to the base-camp to guide the Professor, and bring up another load of necessaries. A cloudless day again, which we employed in making barometrical observations. A light wind from the north-west.

Meanwhile, there are two days for rest in anticipation of unknown hardships ahead—rest which somehow seems sweeter from the thought that to-morrow the remainder of the party will be toiling up the Jones River through cold water and quicksands and thorny woods. But hitherto our rest has not been altogether undisturbed. Curious noises have emanated from the glaciers all around, rumblings and "travelling cracks," which, as the Lieutenant remarked, seemed to go right to the top of Elias and back again. Some of the St. Elias bears are supposed to be of a peculiar grey colour from living constantly like polar bears in "thrilling regions of thick-ribbed ice." The everlasting little avalanches of stones sounded as if they were dislodged by the paws of one of these animals, and made one look up uneasily each time at the moraine. That bears were plentiful and of no insignificant measurements was evident from their tracks upon the wet mud in every direction. One of the party pretended to have been startled from his slumbers by a ridiculous concatenation of noises. He had just composed himself to sleep after saying "good-bye," when, from the steep sides of Mount Vancouver, or of St. Elias, came the distant rumblings of an avalanche. This was followed up by such a series of noises from the Great Guyot Glacier, that it seemed as though something had gone wrong in its internal mechanism. Then a whole troop of St. Elias bears seemed to be flying to our camp for refuge, to judge by the falling stones from the moraine above us. Nearer came the sound and nearer, culminating by the tent door in a loud whirring of wings, till our sleeper's heart "had leaped up into his throat and commenced dangling," as he declared, when there appeared—a tiny humming-bird with iridescent plumage gleaming in the sun, stationary in air, with vibrating wings. A humming-bird in Icy Bay!

This afternoon I made a reconnaissance with Woods, for our journey on the day after to-morrow. I concluded we should have to cross the river somehow, to the other glacier, which was smoother, the ice-mountain-moraine being formed of movable and sharp boulders, and densely overgrown with brushwood and shrubs of beech, birch, and fir. It was an extraordinary spectacle. How far the thicket continued, or where the moraine ceased and the ice came to the surface, was impossible to guess. The highest point visible was 600 feet above the river. The top was evidently moving over the base a few feet daily, and kept rolling trees and stones, as the ice melted, on to the river plain below.

A constant undermining of the base by the river was going on, and milky streams gushed out from half-way up as well as from under the base.

In two hours we approached the spot where the

F

river issued from an ice-cañon, penned in between walls of ice. Icebergs and stranded blocks of ice strewed the banks, others were floating down with the current. A few yards higher up the river issued from under the glacier. The mountain-moraine had bridged it over. The two glaciers had met together and hushed its murmur. A mighty river, as large as the Thames, had disappeared from sight as completely as if it had never existed.

If we can penetrate the brushwood with our packs, we can cross Jones River twenty times over without being aware of its location, as it lies buried under the ice. St. Elias was in sight, and seemed as far away as ever. The sky was clear, but a thick fog-bank hung over the sea, defining exactly the contour of the coast-line.

CHAPTER IV.

Waiting by the Ice—The Indians Return for more Provisions—A vast Moraine overgrown with Trees and Resting upon Moving Ice—Parted from the Guides—Stopped by a Lake of Bergs—We Separate to find a Way—A Dammed-up Torrent Breaks out afresh—Gradual Burial of a Forest Island—Loss of the Professor—Fire, Ice, and Water—We Start again—More Glacial Lakes and the Great Tyndall Glacier—The Fifth Camp reached—Preparations for the Final Ascent.

THE SECOND CAMP, *July 21st,*
Sunset.

WE closed the tents hermetically last night and were not troubled by the mosquitoes. Rose at noon to-day and breakfasted. Weather foggy, and inclined to rain. The four Indians and the Professor arrived at 1 P.M., having taken a shorter way, starting at 7 A.M. He reported that the Indians reached the base-camp at 6 P.M. last night, having clubbed three seals on the way. They had heard shots fired a long distance up the coast, and thought it was a party of Yakatats. We think they are Copper River Indians. The Indians managed to avoid the quicksands this time by wading some channels of the river, but some of the packs got wetted. We hope to make the base of the mountain in three or perhaps in two days.

We have determined to take the barometrical measurements of the altitudes reached over sea-level on our return journey, which is the best way, in case no altitude worth recording is reached.

The Third Camp (on the Ice),
July 22d, Evening.

A fine day. The whole party (as the barometrical observations are to be made on the return) left camp this morning at 6 A.M., having in our packs sufficient for eight days, and making a *cache* of the rest under a mackintosh sheet. Kept alongside the river for some way, having to wade waist-deep in places. The water felt icy-cold, and blocks of ice were floating down the current. Then the Indians struck away through the woods over the moraine. This was a portion of the immense terminal moraine of the "Great Agassiz Glacier" as we named it, which is of enormous extent, and consists of rocks, granite, trachyte, and basalt, and stones, which have fallen, or been torn from the mountain sides, and then carried forward by the constant movement of the ice, till they have collected during the lapse of centuries into a perfect zone of mountains superimposed upon the glacier all along its edges, eight or ten miles in breadth. Under these piles of moving stones, which are for ever being carried forward, lies the glacier ice, three or four hundred feet in thickness at the edge, and much thicker elsewhere; while a tangled forest of spruce and birch, maple and alder, is growing along its extremity, so thickly and closely, that it becomes exceedingly difficult, especially to men with large packs on their backs, to force a way through; as though it were not difficult enough already to walk on loose rocks of every size, varying from that of a house to that of a paving-stone.

But the advancing mass, for it is advancing, is not content with having a forest over it, but it must needs have one under it also, as it gradually covers and buries the narrowing strip of timber. This belt of undergrowth turned out narrower than we expected. It was half a mile only; beyond lay barren moraines or enormous mounds of stones heaped together over the ice and more or less compacted together with age, stretching eastward as far as the eye could reach, and forming the most unpleasant walking imaginable. Morsels of slate, granite, porphyry, felspar, trachyte, and plutonic *débris* were mixed together. The underlying ice very rarely protruded. Here and there lay deep pools of clear water. In the afternoon the Indians, who were behind, twice went off at a tangent in a different direction from that we were taking, without giving any notice of their intention. The second time, they got separated from us by a mile, and the two parties sat on the tops of two moraine mounds making signals which, on account of the distance, we could not understand. The only thing to be done was to exercise a little patience, and soon the proud and stubborn Yakatats found it to be a case of Mahomet and the mountain, and were seen making their way across the glacier to join us, annoyed possibly because they had degenerated from guides to mere porters.

Meanwhile some of the party went prospecting for the best route, as we were shut in and surrounded by badly crevassed portions of the glacier. We had been making for the west flank of a range of hills which seemed the only obstacle to a clear view of the base of St. Elias, which now commenced to tower grandly overhead. This range was not over a mile distant now. The slopes looked

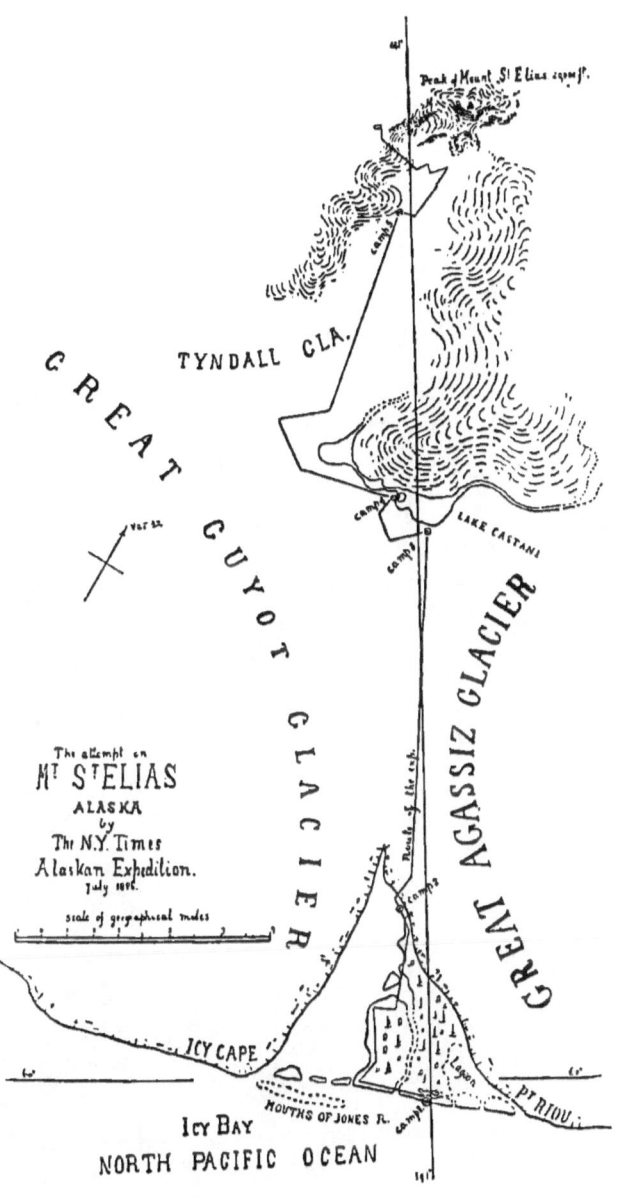

smooth, green, and grassy; the lower parts were timbered. It seemed a forbidden paradise which we were never to reach. The Indians had kept constantly exclaiming that they saw wild mountain goats on it, which was quite impossible at that distance. All day we had been following what seemed the line of junction of two glaciers, with a perceptible depression, as though a river were undermining it. Between us and this range lay what appeared to be a rough ice-surface strewn with *séracs* or small icebergs, and lying lower than the glacier-surface. The searchers came back reporting this to be a lake, and quite impassable. The ice terminated in steep cliffs. It was a lake covered with morsels broken from the glaciers. The only indications of the existence of water was the perfectly flat arrangement of the pieces of ice, which showed they must be floating. Named it after the President of the Italian Geographical Society— Lake Castani.

It was getting dark, and nothing remained except to look for a camping-place on the glacier.

This we found at last on a flat piece of gravel washed down by a stream from the melting ice, like the delta of the Jones River in miniature. The Indians to-night seem ravenously hungry.

THE THIRD CAMP (ON THE ICE),
July 23d, Afternoon.

The next thing to be done was to find a way off the glacier, or at least northward and westward. If we kept on the ice, the road to Mount St. Elias lay to the westward, round the spur or over the lower part of the low range. The Professor thought this way was barred to us on account of the crevasses in the ice, and set out with an Indian this morning in an easterly direction, along the edge of the glacier, to find a way on to the land. I started out with an Indian to the westward with the same object. Both parties agreed to be back by 3 P.M. at latest. It was then 9 A.M.

The crevasses, as I had expected, turned out merely deep corrugations or waves in the surface of the ice, not fissures. The Indian frequently stopped and pointed to his moccasins, which certainly were worn through; but to an Indian accustomed to go barefoot over rough ground what did that signify? However, to induce him to follow, he had to be given a thick pair of woollen socks that I happened to have. To make a long story short, the Indian and I found a way out of the maze or *cul-de-sac* in which the party had found themselves, after two hours fast walking mainly over waves of white ice sprinkled with rocks and stones, with here and there deep mud, on to a small timbered island of thirty acres in extent, situated upon what looked like the damp bottom of a *quondam* lake. It was not, strictly speaking, an island when we reached it, for the lake was, for some reason, below its usual level. This island was bordered on one side by the glacier, which was gradually advancing over it, crushing up the tall pines, rending them into matchwood, and heaping one over the other—a scene of gradual destruction by a resistless force. The onset of the glacier was over-riding and burying the patch of wood. This small island was separated from our low range of hills by a flat expanse of damp gravel, looking like the bed of some mighty torrent the waters of which had been suddenly turned aside into some other channel or dammed up altogether. Subsequently it appeared that the latter was what had taken place.

Cutting off and taking as a proof and sample some green branches, like Noah's dove, we reached camp at one P.M. once more.

By three o'clock the other white man had not returned; but at three-thirty this afternoon the

Indian came back with a note from him saying that he was three hours from camp, and that he fancied a good passage existed across the river which came from the east, but that he had not yet crossed, and that it would take him another hour to do so. Before starting he had agreed to come opposite the camp and fire his rifle and burn a magnesium light, which he thought would be visible a mile away, if he succeeded in crossing. But if there had been found a road to the westward, the fact would be signalled to him by means of the flag we had brought.

Meanwhile the Indians had been grumbling audibly. As translated by Kersunk, the boy interpreter, their mutterings signified that they would prefer going no farther, for their moccasins were worn out. If they were to desert us it might make progress into the interior of the St. Elias alpine region impossible with our heavy packs. But after a little persuasion there suddenly appeared, as if by magic, and from whence it was impossible to say, two new pairs of moccasins.

But the absent one has not returned, so the rest of the party, guided by the Indian who had accompanied me, set off with the packs to the westward by the newly-discovered way, while I am waiting for him with Schwatka.

We have put up the flag-pole. Nothing breaks the silence of the frozen wilderness excepting cracks and groanings in the ice or the roll like distant thunder of an occasional avalanche of snow down the sides of St. Elias (or "ambulance," as the lieutenant called it, *à la Malaprop*), which woke corresponding echoes in the mountains on the west, for there was no wind stirring; or in our more immediate neighbourhood an avalanche of mud, stones, and slush breaking out of some crevice with a rush, and threatening in a miniature way to overwhelm us. Schwatka is seriously ill with a chill, which has brought on fever, ague, and pleuritic pains.

Up till dark we kept examining the glacier with field-glass and telescope, and sweeping the horizon in search of the lost Professor. Then we had dinner—a quarter of a "cracker" apiece,—fireless, for there is no wood.

THE FOURTH CAMP (ON AN ISLAND IN THE ICE),
July 24th, Sunset.

Before we lay down to sleep, towards ten o'clock last night, from a high point on the glacier, a cheering sight was visible, in the shape of an enormous cloud of blue smoke which rose from the spot which Woods and the Indians had reached. Woods was evidently determined that no one else should be given in as "missing," for it rivalled in bulk St. Elias himself. But from the same direction came an incomprehensible sound as of a roaring, rushing torrent, through the still night air. In the morning I had found no sign of such a thing in that direction, only a damp river-bed between the island and the range of hills. Woods had evidently, by the position of the smoke, camped on the island instead of on the range, as we expected he would.

There exists a large river in the direction the Professor has gone, namely, to the eastward, which he has been endeavouring to cross. The one that has meantime burst forth from the westward was even larger. The lake was rising, and it was evident that the two streams united together, and flowing underneath the glaciers along the line of their junction, issued in the form of Jones River at the head of Icy Bay.

At 5.30 A.M. this morning we started for camp, leaving large sheets of newspaper spread out to attract attention, and a note on a stick saying that the absentee was to come on to the smoke of the fires or to wait. On arriving at this camp the bursting forth of a new torrent was confirmed. It was also clear why they had not camped on the range of hills. The new river had been dammed up at some spot above, and was now running " double tides," to make up for lost time. Just as we got into camp, Woods, who had been exploring it, reported a river " big enough to wash away the city of London into the Atlantic Ocean." I could hardly believe it, and went to see. Some alpine lake had burst its bounds. The noise I had heard through the dusk had been the roaring sound caused by rush of many waters contending in their downward course and wrestling as they fell with boulders and blocks of ice.

It seemed as if the forces of nature had combined to prevent our ever reaching St. Elias before our food-supply gave out, not to mention the unfortunate loss of the Professor. Over the waterless channel of yesterday were now surging icebergs down the stream, mixed with roots and trunks of trees. This accounted for the marks of sudden rises and falls in the river-level lower down, and made us fear lest our stores at the second camp should be washed away. Close by, on the banks, an additional guiding-fire which Woods had made had spread over the dry moss. Half a dozen large trees were fairly alight, and sending up such a volume of smoke as must have been visible for fifty miles. The ground wherever it was sandy was covered with tracks of bears, some of which appeared as the impressions of monster paws.

Close by, over the river and looming through the smoke, hung frowning cliffs of ice, the flank of the glacier-face which was burying our island; while, as if to add an additional horror to the scene, a tree crashed down at that moment, overborne by the weight of the advancing glacier. Fire, ice, and water were contending at the same moment in their powers of destruction, and within a distance of a yard or two from each other.

Meantime the four Indians were despatched as two search-parties, with orders to return if they heard two shots fired. Before they had long been gone one party fired two shots for some reason unknown, and the other party of Indians, hearing it, returned to camp, and were again sent out. At 6 P.M this evening, as the lieutenant and I were walking through the timber, a voice cried, "Hello there!" It was the lost one, pale and tired, but safe. He had failed to make his crossing to get off the ice, and had then gone on eastward away from camp with great determination. In the evening, arriving at a lake, he thought a way was possible by making a long *détour*. Shortly after, having slightly sprained his leg, he was unable to make the *détour* to see, but left his gun and instruments on the ice, and walked westward to camp, hoping to meet us coming, and not supposing it to be possible that we had succeeded in finding a way to the eastward. The cloudy pillar had been his guide, but a great many fires had been set blazing, and he had not yet located the one by which our camp was set.

The Fifth Camp (near an Ice-fall at the Foot of Mount St. Elias),
July 25th, 10 P.M.

The Indians who had been searching westward reported finding a good easy way by following the glacier in that direction. This was lucky, as no other way was possible except a retreat. This morning at noon we were once more fairly on the road for St. Elias. The Professor remained behind to connect the camps by simultaneous barometrical readings, having one of the Indians left with him. All carried packs. Only necessaries were taken, including one of the small tents, and all the provisions that could be mustered, rope also and axes. After the vexatious delays, the food could only last us for from four to five days longer.

Keeping up the glacier, over troublesome mounds and hillocks of ice, slightly crevassed and covered several feet in depth with moraine and *débris*, in two hours a flat plateau was reached where the ice gave good walking. In front was another immense glacier; a third stretched away on the left hand side like a plain of ice as far as the eye could reach; while our way opened out plainly by yet another glacier which had its origin from the crags of St. Elias himself.

We soon turned the corner of the range of hills which had offered such an obstacle to us. On the right lay two lakes of muddy water of considerable extent, which were possibly the reservoirs which had become dammed up and had then burst. For nearly two hours longer piles of loose stones were crossed, and the centre of the St. Elias south-west glacier was reached at 5.30 P.M. This we named the Great Tyndall Glacier.

About the centre of it my boots gave out, though I had chosen what I thought were the strongest pair for the last few marches. Our

Indians seemed vastly amused to see a small box of tacks appear from one of their packs, while we mended the refractory boots with the tongue cut out of another boot.

At 8.30 P.M. we left the ice and camped on the last bare slopes anywhere visible, putting up a covey of ptarmigan from it. We were desirous of pressing on and of camping on the ice within a day's reach of the summit, but the Indians' moc-

Mount Cook (16,000 feet) from the Tyndall Glacier.

casins were again worn completely through, while they would in any case from superstitious dread have refused to proceed further.

If the morning turns out fine we intend to start at three o'clock, and, to lose no time, have made up our packs, including two days' provisions and a suit of clothing to wear over the others at night; some Esquimaux coats and hoods of reindeer skin, thirty-five yards of rope, two ice-axes, one alpenstock, one mercurial mountain barometer, one aneroid, one hypsometer, several compasses (one prismatic), two thermometers, and one binocular. The Indians go no farther, the final attack on Mount St. Elias now devolves upon the white men.

CHAPTER V.

The Ascent of Mount St. Elias—Dangerous Crevasses—We are Roped—The Ascent—I reach 6800 Feet over Snow-line—A Bear close to Camp—A Description of the Mountain—The Return to Icy Bay—Quicksands—Three Bears Killed—An Attempt to Launch our Whaleboat through the Surf—We Swamp at Midnight.

THE FOURTH CAMP, *July 27th,*
Sunset.

YESTERDAY we left the last camp at half-past four in the morning for the final ascent. By keeping to the centre of the glacier, which soon turns to the west and runs from thence in a north-easterly direction towards the summit, most of the larger crevasses were avoided. At six it became necessary to rope the party together, as some of the fissures, which now ran transversely, became larger and were partially filled with snow. Joseph Woods the lightest I placed in front, and the lieutenant in the centre as being the heaviest, while I brought up the rear. At this point the boy Frederick, who helped to carry our packs so far, was sent back, and the party consisted then of three.

The clouds had hung heavily, and now commenced closing down. The glacier soon became much cut up. Progress was very slow, and it became necessary to bear away to the west. It soon appeared advisable, as this was the first experience of the other two of any Alpine snow work or of the use of rope and ice-axe, that we should strike off towards one of the ridges on the west, from which several large glaciers descended. Up

Trying to ascend Mount St. Elias.

one of these we now worked in a north-westerly direction. It was in a better condition than the main ice-stream. But as it was now near midday the snow bridges over the fissures were unsafe, and some of the crevasses of great width. It was especially vital to the success of the attempt that the clouds should break and clear away at once. Only three days' food remained in all, while as an additional difficulty, the lieutenant was still seriously ill with fever, and I feared that a night in the snow might even prove fatal to him.

At three the ice was quitted for a slope of crumbling rock with large patches of snow, by which a ridge rising at a steep angle was reached.

Schwatka was now in such an alarming condition from repeated chills, that his state made it necessary to halt for an hour; this delay I took advantage of to make a sketch, before everything was entirely obscured by the mist. Then I resumed the ascent with Woods. At a height of 6800 feet I sent him back to see after Schwatka, and continued the ascent across a narrow snowfield. The upper part of the ridge was swathed in vapour, through which I pressed on till an altitude was reached of almost 7500 feet,* as well as could be computed at the time.

Progress was stopped at 7 P.M., as the ground began to fall away to the west; had the weather been clear, we might have picked out a possible way of ascent even yet, and might even have seen part of the northern face on which no white man's eye at any rate has yet rested.

Compelled by all these "circumstances over

* Subsequently shown to be 7200 feet over sea-level.

which we had no control," we returned to camp, which was at length reached at midnight. I had ascended to a greater height over the summer snow-level than is possible to accomplish in Europe, the snow-level on Mount St. Elias being 400 feet only above the sea-level owing to the heavy annual snow-fall.

The day before, we had told the Indians that our stock of provisions was very small, requesting them to eat but little. We found they had left untouched the whole that remained, regaling themselves on wild roots and water. As we could remain no longer, a good meal and light packs were the order of the day; especially for the Indians, whose capability for either fasting or repletion is very great. Before leaving, Woods, who had left the hypsometer a short distance from camp, had to return for it. As he was coming down the bed of a stream he saw a large grey-coloured bear, evidently one of the Elias grizzlies. The 50-calibre Winchester had been left in the last camp. The bear seemed to be eating the wild or "skunk" cabbage, and took no notice whatever, and probably did not see Woods.

I subsequently went to look at the bear. It was a large brute, and I longed for some weapon of offence. Woods also killed four ptarmigan with an ice-axe. These birds evidently had broods, and were most pugnacious, following like dogs, and running round and round us with outspread wings. They were welcome as a supply of meat. We reached the camping-ground at seven this evening. The Indians declared they felt the ground moving and shaking as they lay in their "lean-to." If it was not mere imagination, the lieutenant was shivering and shaking from chills and fever with almost sufficient violence to convey the sensation of an earthquake to the acute senses of the Indians.

During the intervals of clear weather there have been many opportunities of sketching and examining Mount Saint Elias, both with telescope and binocular as well as with the naked eye, from our various camps and stopping-places from different points of view. A description would be of interest in view of future attempts to climb the mountain. Its height has been differently estimated by the old navigators, Cook, Vancouver, Tebenkoff, La Perouse, Bering, and Belcher, and it is the only mountain the real height of which has exceeded the first estimates made of it. Mountains generally prove lower than they were originally believed to be, but the latest determination taken from

Yakatat and from the U.S. Coast Survey schooner, *Yukon*, gives 19,500 and possibly 20,000 feet. It certainly, from its massive shape, gives the impression of being less than this, notwithstanding that its whole altitude is presented to the eye, from its sharp summit down to the ocean at its foot. The northern ridge of the pyramid, as seen from the same spot in profile, presented the same angle of descent as the southern ridge—about forty-five degrees. Something in the shape of Elias from Yakatat reminds one of Piz Roseg as seen from the Roseg Glacier.

The first features that fix the attention are the outline as seen from Icy Bay, being a reproduction on a slightly larger scale of Mount Fairweather; next that Elias forms a regular quadrilateral pyramid; next the detached circular crater-like basin nearly half-way up the central front; next the regularity of three of the pyramidal side ridges and the assumption that the fourth ridge must be equally regular; and fifthly, the solitary and isolated situation of the Ice King—the terminating and crowning elevation of his range, so close upon the sea—the highest peak[*] in North America gazing out over the

---

[*] Lieutenant Allen asserts that Mount Wrangel, lying at the forks of the Copper River, is even higher.

widest ocean of the world. But though so like in shape to Fairweather, which is 15,500 feet, there exists a difference, in that the two ridges which appear like shoulders or wings on each side of the two summits, in Elias are longer, while the eastern shoulder is lower than the western. In Fairweather both are of equal height. The four arêtes or ridges appear to run north, south, east, and west. The north-west face of the mountain has never been seen. The north-east face seemed from Yakatat to consist of steep cliffs. The east ridge descends from the summit as a snow arête with a gradually decreasing rapidity for about 4000 feet, forming one of the before-mentioned shoulders; from which point it falls in cliffs of steep black rock with one break, a depression holding a small hanging glacier.

Next comes the south-east face. The upper triangular part consists of steep slopes of rock and snow, and the lower part of perpendicular precipices. The sharp contrast between the black and the white, the rock and snow; and the well-defined line of demarcation, half way up, between snow-field and precipice, forms a marked feature of this face.

Then the central or south ridge of the pyramid slopes at an angle of forty-five degrees from the summit to a depression lying seven or eight thousand feet below it, between the mountain and the crater-basin. This crater, for such it appears, though we found no volcanic traces on the moraine, should be from four to five thousand feet in diameter. It lies in front of, and separate from, the main volume of the mountain, and about midway between base and summit. The encircling ridge encloses it on three sides only, leaving the interior open to view on the south-east. The inner cliffs of the crater descend too steeply to allow snow to rest on them, but enclose four hanging glaciers. On the outside of the crater are five other glaciers, and between them four ridges descending to the main glacier at the foot, which seem accessible half way up—two of them even look easy—whence the rim of the crater could be reached. From this point it appears that the main snow-fields on the south-west face might be attained.

On the south-west side, from the summit of Elias, the snow and rock, very steep at first, stretches down at a gradually lessening angle to a plateau of *névé*, which winds down towards the crater, then turns from behind it to the westward, being much crevassed, and descends at an angle of about twenty degrees to the main glacier, which we named the

Great Tyndall Glacier, which now flows to the south-east along the foot of the mountain, past the base of the crater, where it widens and turns to the south. At this point, where *névé* and glacier mingle, and which may be called the source of the main southern Elias Glacier, some tributary glaciers flow in and join from the westward; while between this point and the crater are two fine ice-falls. In the centre of the south-west face a long regular and sharp ridge joins the main mass of Elias, and divides the above-mentioned sloping plateau of *névé* into two.

This sharp ridge has also the effect of partly hiding the western edge of the Elias pyramid, which, as I could see from the highest point reached, trended somewhat to the northward in its lower part, and promised, on the whole, a not impracticable way of ascent. Reaching the west shoulder would be identical with reaching the summit itself. While the sky in this direction appeared to us generally more free from those clouds and masses of fog which were so prevalent just at the period when their absence was so important to us, and which caused us so much trouble and annoyance. In this direction the "foot-hills" of Elias stood like islands in the enormous expanse of glacier stretching prairie-like as far as the eye could penetrate through the crystalline air towards the country of the Atna or Copper River; and in the same direction was seen another lofty range standing near the sea, and completely enshrouded and enveloped in the ice from which it rose, and on which it seemed, so to speak, to rest or float as on an ocean. But while the sky in the north-west was more favourable, a constant canopy of fog-bank hung over the sea at times, ending abruptly with the land, and thus defining the coast-line, especially Yakatat Bay.

Returning now to the foot of the crater, the main glacier at this point is approximately six miles in width, and, as stated before, now flows southward to the ocean, bounded by ranges of snowy hills which contribute numerous streams of ice to swell its volume. This we named the Tyndall Glacier, and it was our pathway going to and returning from our last camping place.

These boundary ranges to this glacier, which divide it from the vast ice-plains on the east and west of it, cease at a distance of twenty miles from Mount Elias. It then widens out and mingles with the seas of ice and moraine, which cost us three days to cross, and which form the shores of Icy and

Yakatat Bays; while an immense ice-river, twenty miles broad and of unknown length, comes in from the westward (which we called the Great Guyot Glacier), and where, as we could see from the greatest elevation reached, were endless ice-fields. Towards Yakatat also, a plain of glacier stretches for fifty miles, which must comprise 700 square miles; the seaward part consists of moraines, of course underlaid with ice. The U.S. Coast Survey named this Malaspina, as being apparently "a plateau bare of vegetation," and a "*buried glacier.*" It is, however, not exactly "bare of vegetation," for so slow is the glacier's march, and so huge are the mountains of moraine that border it, that large parts are covered with thick bush, through which it is difficult to penetrate.

It would probably be below the mark to give 10,000 square miles as the area of the glaciers between Mount Elias and the Copper River country, and 8000 from Elias eastward, and southward to Cross Sound, making 18,000 square miles of glaciers, while merely those which border the shore must comprise an area of about 2500 square miles of rough but level fields of ice.

TABLE OF HEIGHTS.

Everest (in the Himalayas), 29,002 feet (snow-line from 15,500 to 18,000 feet).
Aconcagua (in the Andes), 23,000 (snow-line, 12,780).
Chimborazo, 21,420.
A summit in the Hindu Kush, 20,593.
Mount St. Elias, 19,000 to 20,000 (U.S. Coast Survey's observations).
Cayembe, 19,625.
Kilimanjaro, approximately, 19,000.
Tolima, 18,314.
Kara Korum Pass (Himalayas), 18,200.
Elburz (Caucasus), 17,800.
Mount Cook, 16,000.
Mount Brown (British Columbia), 16,000.
Mount Crillon, 15,900.
Mount Murchison (British Columbia), 15,789.
Mont Blanc, 15,784.
Mount Hooker (British Columbia), 15,700.
Mount Fairweather, 15,500.
Monte Rosa, 15,223.
Mount Tacoma (Oregon), 14,440.
Mount Adams (Washington Territory), 13,258.
Mount Vancouver, 13,100.
The Gross Glockner (Tyrol), 12,956.
The Adler Pass, 12,461.
Mount Cook (New Zealand), 12,460.
Muley Hacen (Spain), 11,664.
Col du Geant, 11,426.
Mount La Perouse, 11,300.
Mount Hood (Oregon), 11,220.
Mount Maladetta (Pyrenees), 11,168.
Ischar Dagh (Balkans), 10,000.
Ruska Poyano (Carpathians), 9912.
Monte Corno (Apennines), 9523.
Highest in Arabia, 8593.

Snæ Hattan (Norway), 8102.
Kosciuska (Australia), 6500.
Alleghany Mountains (North Carolina), 6476.
Ben Nevis, 4406.
The Catskills, 4000.
Snowdon, 3590.

The Second Camp, *July 28th*,
9 P.M.

Made the whole distance to-day from the fourth camp. The water is two feet higher. We knew the river would rise after the sudden appearance of a torrent, where I had found nothing but bare ground the day before. Though in peril, the *cache* we had left was safe; the Professor had been using some of the provisions, and had evidently left only that morning for the base camp, after having shifted the things out of harm's way, for the ashes of his camp fire were still warm.

Icy Bay. The Base Camp,
July 29th, Sunset.

Leaving the second camp at seven this morning we abandoned everything not absolutely needed. We had to keep through thick wood away from the river for the first mile, on account of the high state of the water. The quicksands were covered where we had crossed previously; but in another place we waded breast-high in the river, which had a shifting sandy bottom. Struck more quicksands on the other side. Here the lieutenant sank up to his middle, and was pulled out with the end of an alpenstock. He says he struck bed-rock. If we had only known this before, how boldly we should have allowed ourselves to sink, and with what nonchalance crossed the very worst places. The last river was also breast-high. Reached this camp at 3 P.M., and found that Dalton had killed three bears on the beach near by. He informed us that it had rained daily. The biggest bear had sat up and looked at him, and had crawled a hundred yards after being shot. The Professor struck a bad part of the river in crossing the quicksands, and his Indian dropped and lost everything that was not tied on.

Icy Bay. The Base Camp,
July 30*th, Midday.*

All day yesterday we rested, watched the surf, listened to the roar of the ocean, and wondered how we were going to get away. We determined to try to get away by that night's tide. It was high water at about 11.30 P.M. We packed the things, leaving most of the remaining provisions, and other things that were not indispensable. Towards sundown everything had been carried across the sand dunes to the side of the whale-boat. Oars and mast were made ready and everything prepared. *Breakers* were filled and *rollers* laid, the very names conveying unpleasant reminders. The anchor had been thrown out as far as possible by Woods wading out at five that afternoon at low water, when the Indian canoes are said to be able to make a landing.

Still the length of cable we had to haul on to get through the breakers looked miserably short and insufficient, and threatened that we should be unable to take quick advantage of the calm moment on account of the difficulty of raising the anchor, which, as well as the chain, sinks in a few minutes to a great depth in the sand. How deep would it sink in six hours? The last twenty yards are of chain, and this, as well as the anchor, was very heavy, making it slow and hard work moving it. I advised not using them. The pile of *impedimenta* looked formidable, and were packed into the boat to occupy the smallest space. As midnight approached we made ready. We took off our boots and coats, and stood round the boat to hold firm as the foam rushed by. It was icy cold to legs and feet; and uniting our strength, we moved her down upon the underwash of each succeeding wave.

We had suspected that the boat was too heavily loaded for nine men to manage, and too low to give her the necessary chance of rising over the foaming breakers, comparatively small though they were when contrasted with those of winter.

But most of the scientific instruments were the private property of one of the members of the party, and were valuable. We were therefore unwilling to abandon them to their fate. To make the situation more unpleasant it was nearly midnight and the darkness was increasing. Our legs were numbed; for the many glacial rivers and the glaciers along the shore made the water bitterly cold. The waves seemed getting larger. It was spring-tide. Soon an enormous breaker came on like a wall, and broke with a roar like thunder. The foam rushed up the beach towards us. Now was the time. We gasped for breath in the icy water, and held firm to the boat till the wave began to retreat again. "All together now" some one shouted, and exerting our full strength we rushed her down a few yards on the retiring flood.

We were now nearer to danger than ever. Some water had entered the boat over the gunwales already. The sand seemed to hold her sucked down. The canoe had been tied behind with twenty yards of rope. We had seen it rush past us caught by the back sweep of the water, and next moment become broken into small pieces which floated uncomfortably round about, like an entanglement, till some one cut the rope adrift. We were watching the next opportunity—a retreating underwash followed by calm water for a moment. The Indians strained their eyes seawards. Everything was obscured by the darkness, for it was past midnight. We had calculated on its being lighter. Now—now was the time, and a yell arose from the whole party. Next minute we were completely enveloped in foam, as we struggled to keep a footing, gasping from the cold. The rush of water was terrific. It seemed like a nightmare enacted by madmen. Wave succeeded wave till she was filled and immovable. Everything became confusion. Behind was a desert, in front the roaring sea in which our effects were at the point of destruction, while the surf breaking upon us chilled us through and through. We were between the devil and the deep sea, and the devil received the vote, for "back" was now the cry. We were defeated and cast once more upon an inhospitable shore. Four held the boat, while the rest carried package after package above the reach of the waves.

Shouts for assistance were heard as the waves got the better of the four, and "slewed her broadside;" till bailed out and dragged up she was made fast for the present out of reach of the tide. So ended our first attempt to leave Icy Bay. Here we are still. We have still some provisions left, and must make one last desperate effort if the surf remains moderate. The matches were dry, and a hot fire and coffee were cheering, as were also the few blankets that remained dry.

The roaring of the surf kept every one awake till the sun was high in the heavens, reminding us as it did that calmer weather was the only alternative to capsizing or semi-starvation; while the brightest star in the mental atmosphere is the return of the man-of-war in a month.

To-day the weather is clear and cloudless, the mirage along the shore rising and falling as the wind drifts the spray from the breaking surf inland. The beach is strewed with things laid out to dry; luckily it is a fine warm day.

CHAPTER VI.

A Fresh Attempt to Pass the Surf of Icy Bay—Abandonment of our Possessions—Skirting the Shore—Crossing Yakatat Bay—We camp by the Indian Village—Haggling with the Natives, or "Chin-music"—Our Life at Yakatat—An Attempt to Recover the Abandoned Property—The Kaiak Traders arrive in their Schooner—Poisoning of the Indians with Arsenic—Murder of George Holt—The Chief Medicine-Man—I leave Yakatat—The *New York Times* Expedition waits for the Man-o'-War—Becalmed—Shooting Seals—A Sea-otter Hunt—Cape Yagtag—A Wild Stern Coast-line—Another enormous Glacier—Life on the Schooner—Cape Suckling—Cape Martin—Kaiak Island.

YAKATAT BAY, *August 2d,* 1886.

FRESH preparations for departure were begun. The anchor and chain were extracted from the sand and laid thirty yards farther out at low water, favoured by the spring-tide, by Woods and Dalton, after a violent struggle with the waves. It grew gradually calmer; our expectations rose. The scientific instruments were heavy; must the Professor leave them? No, they must be taken in the cause of science. If we were destined to swamp, we should swamp without them as easily as with them. The Indians were consulted; they would start at daybreak on the ebbing tide. It grew calmer still. If it should only keep so for eight hours longer! At all hazards we must break through the bounds of our prison-house.

The surf broke in long straight lines, every portion simultaneously. The sound of it was louder, but the sea in reality calmer. Each roller was clearly defined from each succeeding one. We could pick out the moment for the last rush with certainty. It was 7 o'clock in the evening. We lay down, and each one feigned sleep, but no one slept. We were face to face with a danger, but we talked of other things. The Indians watched the sea by turns all night, and roused Dalton to prepare breakfast as the first light of morning lit the sky behind the vast ranges of alps. Almost everything was abandoned this time. The boat was therefore nearly empty.

The air was thick with sea fog, but the sea was still in good condition. It grew lighter and lighter. Everything is ready, and away we go down the beach. Now she touches the wash. We haul in the slack of the anchor rope and bide our time. Determination is imprinted on every face. The undemonstrative Indians get really excited and show it. We leave it to them to give the word. The glaciers make the sea almost icy cold, and we shudder as each surge breaks and rushes under us. The moment arrives when we see a calm stretch. "All together!" and she moves seaward. Now she floats. Pull on the anchor rope for life or death. "Jump in, boys!" "Row, for God's sake, row!" The chain is caught in the sand and refuses to come up. Some one cuts the rope. All is confusion. The oars are entangled and refuse to enter the rowlocks. "Row, for God's sake, row!" At last I get one in, and a wave strikes it out again. (I found afterwards this rowlock was bent.) She surges to and fro. Nothing at this moment could take my attention from the rowlock, though it were to rain "chained thunderbolts and hail of iron globes." I wrestle with my oar, and everything beside passes unheeded except the cry dinning in one's ears, "Row, for God's sake, row!" A small wave passes under her and breaks just under the keel; she turns broadside. Has no one got an oar out? Ten yards more and we shall be safe. I seize another oar; some one is sitting upon it. I try another, and the stay catches. At last one oar is got to work; then another. Every one shouts at once. Never was seen such confusion, or heard such pandemonium. Hades must have broken loose. The importance of the next few seconds is immense. At last she moves—faster and faster— no heavy sea yet. We are safe. No! look out— yes, safe at last. An immense roller arrives. She rises to it, and it passes under and breaks just beyond us. The shore recedes. We are soaked through and through, but safe. We are exhausted, and can afford to rest. We bail the boat, and change into dry things which we have taken care to place in rubber bags. The fog lifts. Never did Mount St. Elias look so grand, so magnificent. Our deserted tent stands lonely on the shore. It shows white against the dark narrow belt of forest, which in its turn shows up blackly against the glittering sea of glaciers beyond.

We have the best boat from the man-of-war. We can set no sail, for not a breath moves the glassy surface of the Pacific, yet we can row her at a rate of four knots. We taste the water and find it fresh.

We pass along the coast, keeping well clear of the line of breakers. In a few hours we reach Point Sitkagi, the thin line of swamp and timber ends, and we skirt mile after mile of brown-looking ice-cliffs where the Great Agassiz

Glacier reaches the sea. Piles of moraine rubble and stones lies on its upper surface; streams of water issue from its cracks and fissures and flow down its face into the ocean.

At midday we are abreast of the point called Manby by the coast survey; it only remains to cross the Bay of Yakatat, a distance of twenty miles, and about sixty from the starting-point.

At Point Manby some belts of timber fringe the coast line, which continue for ten miles up the bay, when the ice-cliffs recommence. In front of the timber stretches the same long straight line of sand, backed by a ridge of gravel and stones which allow only the tree tops to be seen beyond, and on which the Pacific surf breaks ceaselessly— clearly a shore not intended for man to land upon.

A breeze springs up, and the sail is hoisted. Quantities of seal "bob up serenely" all round, as many as fifteen glistening black heads at once, and disappear again in the thick white water. They are the common hair-seals, and this is an Indian seal-hunting ground.

Ocean Cape and Cape Phipps soon rise into view. Each fir-tree becomes defined, and the coast line presents a serrated edge. The Indian village comes in sight. The chief hoists his flag on the flag-pole, and the natives crowd on the roofs of the houses. As we draw up on the beach, crowds of Yakatat Indians, men, women, and naked children, surround us. They have returned, since we left, from seal-hunting. Most of them have their faces painted black or red, and stare intently and silently without one of them offering to help us.

We pitch camp on the sandbank, now denuded of strawberries by the newly-arrived inhabitants, fetching our second large tent and boxes from the chief's house, where they have been stored. We find the chief seated on a magnificent bear robe by the side of his wife and daughter, and wearing his uniform and the U.S.S. *Pinta* riband. The crowd fills the house and still pours in by the small circular opening called a door. The smoke ascends through a hole in the roof, across which are hung strings of dried salmon and salmon-trout.

After much talk, we tell the chief in reply that though we have not actually reached the summit of the big mountain, we have ascended higher above the snow-line than any other living men.

YAKATAT BAY, *August 3d.*

The chief visited us yesterday in camp at supper, and ate some pilot bread and bacon. Rows of brown naked children, with black beady eyes, sit round four deep and watch every operation with an intense and speechless interest.

The bedding having been left at Icy Bay, we have to use a supply of new blankets we stored here. This morning our Indians were paid in trading material, which they chose for themselves out of the supply brought.

YAKATAT BAY, *August 5th,* 1886.

The last two days have been consumed in bargaining with the Indians in trading material for curios (such as masks and arrows, spoons of wild sheep and goat horns, charms, carved bones, and baskets woven out of roots and grass), but in a manner tedious and trying to the patience. Besides salmon, and occasionally a small halibut, the Indian squaws have been daily bringing clams, cockles, crabs, and baskets of strawberries, salmon-berries, and blueberries. The Alaskan climate produces a fine appetite, and with Dalton, Woods, and Frederick, the cooking is a marvel. One is liable to eat too much, and disinclined in consequence to do anything but lie in the tent.

All the same, the Professor seems not to be affected in that way, since he has set up an observatory in a perforated deal box, screwed to a stump, with wind gauges, barometers, thermometers, and other instruments.

The Indians do not venture near, for they consider it must be "big medicine."

The Professor.

I made a sketch in oils yesterday of the chief's daughter. Several men were asked first to sit, and all showed some reluctance, so I was surprised to find the chief willing to allow his daughter to do so. She is about fifteen years of age, and came escorted by her husband and father-in-law, as well as by the chief and his wife. I had to make brushes out of bits of rope, the others being at Icy Bay. I kept her sitting an hour, and gave her a looking-glass.

Eight Indians have consented to go to Icy Bay in large canoes and endeavour to recover the things left there, saying they might have long to wait for an opportunity of launching the canoes to return. They start immediately. One of them, who owns a partly ruined hut there, is bold looking, with an honest and trustworthy as well as picturesque appearance. He is one of the only two men who hunt bears in this neighbourhood; the other is one of our Indians, "the hunter," as we called him. Some may remain the whole winter, for there are plenty of seals there, as we discovered.

Yesterday the trader's schooner, of about twenty tons burden, arrived from Kaiak Island, and is now lying at anchor. They have offered to take the whole party to their store at Kaiak, whence we can reach Nuchuk in canoes, where a schooner belonging to the Alaska Commercial Company will call in September. By this we could reach Kodiak, and thence San Francisco, by the steamer *St. Paul*.

I have accepted their offer. The others prefer to remain at Yakatat until the man-of-war arrives to take them back to Sitka. To-day we had an exhibition of fireworks and athletics. The best man among the Indians wrestled with Dalton.

YAKATAT BAY, *August 9th.*

On the evening of the 6th a great beating of drums and sticks, which continued nearly all night, was heard in the village. The noise seemed to issue from the last house. It was broken at times by the howling of the wolf-like dogs which swarm, and yell in chorus like coyotes, generally clustering together for the purpose on some promontory or lonely and distant spot.

We sallied out in a body to see what was doing. The interior of the house was lit up by the firelight. The *shawaan* was seated, naked to the waist, performing incantations and machinations over a sick child, though the child itself was nowhere visible. His long hair, always left uncut, was streaming behind him. He was shaking his charms, throwing his body into contortions, uttering shrill cries, hissing and extending his arms, groaning and breathing through his clenched teeth, jerking himself meantime in convulsive starts in cadence to the music. Seated round the fire, a dozen Yakatat Indians were beating drums and pieces of wood together, keeping time to the jerks of the *shawaan's* head and body. This old medicine-man is quite blind, having been deprived of his sight in a fight with another medicine-man.

Next morning some Yakatat women came to the tent ostensibly to trade some curios. Their real object was different. They had brought with them one of our baking-powder tins, which contained a white powder, and which they thought must be "no good," for all the Indians who had eaten of bread baked with this powder were now lying ill; some of them being Sitkans, besides our guide, Bear Hunter, and his family.

A Yakatat Medicine-Man.

The Professor recognised the powder, which was pure arsenic. While at Icy Bay, Dalton had taken some of the drug (used for preserving objects of natural history) to poison a bait for foxes half a mile from camp at the head of the lagoon, and had carelessly utilised a baking-powder tin for carrying the poisonous mineral. One of the Indians had found the tin near the line of march; it was promptly taken

I

from him by the Professor and given to Dalton to be destroyed. He had, however, merely hidden it. The same Indian, with his thievish propensities, had sought it out again, concealing it this time in another Indian's bundle, who had brought it with him to Yakatat (to cause misery, illness, and subsequently death to three persons). To pick up and make use of articles discarded or thrown away as useless is an unconquerable habit with the Alaskan Indian.

Mr. Schwatka, in his western experiences on the plains, has known instances where the pernicious stuff has been the cause of deaths amongst a hunting party by a precisely similar mistake.

As the medicine chest was among the things at Icy Bay, nothing could be done but to recommend hot salt water immediately as an emetic. The Professor endeavoured to superintend, but was not allowed even to use one of their kettles for fomentations for fear of contamination with the sick.

The morning wore on, and no Indians came to trade. At length Frederick brought word that a child was dead, and that one of the Indians and his wife, who had refused the emetic, were seriously ill, but that all who had taken it were recovering.

At intervals a distant drumming and yelling from the interior of the houses told us that the *shawaan* was busy at his work. The chief came and went, and the deplorable conduct of the Indian, among those now at Icy Bay, was fully explained to him.

Meanwhile we all visited the Indian houses to see if anything further could be done, and sent to inform the traders of the state of affairs. They soon came across in their "dory." Calms and contrary winds had given them a long passage from Kaiak. The only item of news they could give us was of the murder by an Indian of George Holt, the storekeeper at the Company's store at the Knik River in Cook's Inlet. News had been sent of the occurrence to San Francisco, and it was hoped that the Government would take the necessary steps for the capture of the murderer. Having been turned out of the store by Holt for misbehaviour, he had laid in wait for him and shot him in the back next day. This post on the Knik River has usually been abandoned during the summer months for an island in the estuary on account of the mosquitoes. The Indians arrive to trade from the interior mostly during winter.

On Board the Schooner *Three Brothers,*
August 9th, *Sunset.*

This morning we were up early and saw a thick column of smoke rising from the village. They were cremating the body of the child. The usual sounds of drumming were issuing from the chief's house, where the sick people are lying. Entering the house, we found the blind *shawaan* again at his tricks. He was squatting by the side of our Indian, who was evidently better, for he was vomiting, having at length taken the emetic. The *shawaan* was neglecting the wife, and devoting his magic arts exclusively to the husband.

Sitting down, I commenced to sketch the sightless savage, who, of course, was unaware that I was drawing him. The chief kept telling me not to be afraid, for he was blind. Perhaps he thought as I had sketched his daughter that it would prevent any ill effects if I did the same to the *shawaan*. Presently he stripped himself, and opening his box of charms, took out a wooden figure of a crane with a frog clinging to its back, and a bunch of sea-otter's teeth and carved walrus tusks. The latter he placed on the naked stomach of the dying man.

Meantime the drums and sticks kept up the

monotonous noise, and the heat and stench were increased by the fire. The *shawaan* grew more excited. His contortions and jerks grew more and more active. His favourite attitude seemed to be with the right arm drawn up, and hand half-clenched under the ear, the left arm extended, squatting in Eastern fashion, the body crouched and greasy with oil and the heat.

At a sign his hair was uncoiled and unknotted by the assistant-magician. Its length was at least five feet, but might possibly have been added to artificially. At times in his leaps and jerks the ends came perilously near the fire. He seemed aware of this, for he occasionally drew them in. Every few minutes, too, white eagles' down was held between finger and thumb by the assistant, and blown over his head and shoulders, to which it adhered, giving hair and skin a hoary and ancient look, or as though he was covered with freshly fallen snow-flakes. The dying man paid but little regard to him, and before many hours had elapsed both he and his wife had passed away.

Disgusted by the sight, and sickened by the stench, I sought the air, and saw a flag flying from the schooner's mainmast—a sign to come on board, for there was a fair wind. The sails were hoisted as an additional sign, in case the flag should have passed unnoticed. After a hurried leave-taking I rowed on board, only to find the breeze dying out. It rose again, though faintly; so the anchor was weighed, and she put to sea. Some hours later, as she lay idle and becalmed barely two miles from land, the sails flapping as she rose and fell, a canoe shot out from the promontory containing the chief and his wife. They had come to beg! As the little schooner lay becalmed they thought it a good opportunity to do so, unobserved by the rest of the tribe.

ON BOARD THE SCHOONER *Three Brothers of Kodiak*, *August 10th, Mid-day.*

We are becalmed off Icy Bay, having made small progress, with only "light airs;" but the breeze, such as it is, is now right aft.

August 11th.

We were favoured by a light but fair breeze yesterday afternoon, and with the assistance of the current, which sets continually to the westward, we have made forty miles. At the same time a thick black cloud hung over the sea, some of the rain from which reached us. There was also a flash of lightning and some thunder—very rare phenomena in these parts, and the first the Carlsens had heard—but the sky was perfectly clear to the eastward. Seals were numerous, and the steersman, either William or Nils, who took it in turns, kept firing as we went along. Seal meat is quite palatable, though seal blubber is exceedingly fishy to the taste. But at 3 P.M. a sea-otter made his appearance, and all our rifles were got out and several shots fired, but at a long range, and without any result.

At 6 P.M. we were all in the cabin when another alarm was given by the steersman. Another sea-otter had been seen close alongside. It was raining hard, but a long fusillade commenced. Twice it gave a fair opportunity, coming to the surface to breathe close to the schooner. Some bullets had struck the sea close by the animal, which appeared to have been wounded, as its movements were slow and uncertain. The schooner was put about four or five times as the otter dodged and came up now in front and now on the right or left. Each time the creature rose some one fired, to make it dive and so exhaust it, for the sea-otter is a warm-blooded animal, and must come to the surface every few minutes to breathe.

After a time it remained floating three hundred

yards astern (a seal shows only its head, or head and flipper, but a sea-otter shows its whole length), and no further firing would make the animal dive, unless the bullets were exceedingly close. It was difficult to make even fair shooting on account of the motion of the vessel, while the wind having dropped, it was impossible to follow up the chase by putting about.

As there seemed no promise of the breeze getting up again, the men launched the "dory" to continue the pursuit, leaving me to manage the schooner alone, and to signal to them from the deck in which direction to row, the view thence being more extensive than from the "dory."

By this time the sea-otter had recovered his breath, and his next appearance was so distant that the chase was given up. While it lasted it was exciting, and an immense number of cartridges were consumed.

We were now opposite a point on the coast where a party of Indians which had been fitted out by the traders with boats and guns had been landed to hunt sea-otters. This was where the glacier which projects and forms the west side of Icy Bay terminates, after sweeping or curving round to the west, at the foot of a low range of hills. The ridges of these hills are covered with glacier ice, which pours down the ravines and sides in a series of frozen cascades.

The landing is said to be partially protected by a low sand ridge or point which exists. The traders had always known this landing by the name of Icy Bay landing. As we passed by the slight indentation forming the true Icy Bay of the charts, twenty miles back, I had pointed out to them our deserted tent, just visible with the naked eye, as we were four or five miles off shore. It stood out like a shining, square, white speck upon that grand and awful coast in relief against the narrow belt of forest.

Meanwhile nothing was seen of the traders' hunting party who were to have come out to us to be taken back to Kaiak in the schooner. They must have heard the firing, and had not the surf prevented them, would have put off. As the swell was not formidable, it was evident they had already returned. From the east cape of Icy Bay, called Icy Cape, where the glacier projects farthest into the sea, to this point, a distance of five or six miles, the ice presents a high serrated wall to the ocean, and differs from the other ice fronts which fringe the coast, and which are of a dirty drab colour, from the moraines and sand heaps superimposed upon them, in that here the ice is a pure greenish-white, and falls abruptly in peaked and jointed terraces. The front of the glacier is a cliff which "beetles o'er his base into the sea," which thunders below. It is the sea front of the Great Guyot Glacier, washed and broken by the Pacific surge.

Towards sunset we lay rising and falling slowly in the long waves off the Cape Yagtag of the charts, where a reef of rocks is said by the Indians to act as a slight protection to the beach. From here westward " the foot-hills," as it were, of Elias fringe the coast line, timbered at the lower levels with firs. Their feet are bathed in a stratum of sea-mist rising from the Pacific surf, which bursts and dies without cessation; and from the long booming line of foam rises for ever its ghost, in the shape of spray and vapour, which rolls away like smoke, and half conceals the trees in a veil of rainbow colours, and hangs over the ice like a cold white pall.

All along the sides and summits of these hills, in every hollow and in every possible and impossible position, lie glaciers of all sizes, connected and disjointed, large and small. Here and there lie patches of snow and broad fields of *névé*. Wherever the gravelly or sedimentary deposits of which the mountains are composed protrude through the ice or snow, they are of a warm red-brown colour. As we lie on the glassy and heaving surface, I can just see the summit of St. Elias over a dip in the range. This dip is filled up by a glacier which seems to come rushing and pouring down the valley to the sea like a Niagara of ice. From here the higher slopes of Elias look harmlessly easy. The western ridge appears to fall away gently to the north, and to offer a practicable way of ascending the mountain.

I had understood that with Icy Cape the last ice along the coast line was left behind. But looming twenty miles or so to the westward appears another vast ice-plain, to which I ventured to give a name,[*] and which sweeps down and opens fan-like on the ocean, where the coast range of "foot-hills" comes to an end. It is evidently the opening or outlet of the vast glacier-desert or ice-lake which we saw from the slopes of Mount St. Elias, lying to the north-west of that mountain. Its birthplace is an icy range that forms an enlarged continuation of the great western ridge of Elias. It is not marked or

[*] Proceedings of the Royal Geographical Society, May 1887.

mentioned by the early navigators, all of whom mistook the true nature of these stupendous glaciers, La Perouse describing them as "snow lying upon a barren soil," and "a plain totally destitute of verdure."

A blue range of hills on the coast beyond is Cape Suckling, just off which, but not yet visible, lies Kaiak Island, the traders' post, and their present home.

Occasionally the black shining head of a seal offered a difficult mark, and a shot was fired at it. Then a line was baited with a piece of salt salmon and let down for a chance halibut.

The three men each have a share in the schooner. Having a good understanding with the Alaska Commercial Company, they have set up a store at Yakatat Bay, and another at Kaiak, but the natives are not great fur-hunters at these places, and their most profitable trips are made on behalf of the Company. One of them cooks meals with the small stove in the cabin, and is exempted in consequence from night-watches—tea and coffee, salt salmon, bread and butter, and "mush," being the usual fare, varied with "Cape Horn fry," or a can of California honey.

Three Miles from Kaiak Island,
August 13th, 10 a.m.

Yesterday a smart south-west breeze sprung up at mid-day, and continued all the afternoon, blowing very fresh by evening, and aggravating the Pacific swell. It was dead ahead, but better than a calm. We tacked against it steadily. On the south tack the schooner pitched a good deal, but we stood to sea till land was ten miles distant. But once again, at 7 p.m., it fell calm, so the "dory" was launched to tow, while the two long sweeps were

The St. Elias Alps, the third highest range in the world, viewed from the westward.

used from the deck. When all hands turned in, after three hours' work, she hardly seemed to have advanced much.

Kaiak was still twenty-five miles distant. By sunrise we had made five miles. After breakfast the sweeps were got out, and with the help of light airs we made considerable way again. Cape Suckling was now full in view, and appeared to consist of two rocky wooded points running out into the sea and terminating in red cliffs. Behind them a range of hills, with bare, bright-green summits, runs back ten or twelve miles. On each side lie low land, sand-bars, lagoons, and forest flats. This strip of verdant land, like an oasis in the wilderness, is cut off and imprisoned on the inland side by the interminable plains of glaciers that my eye was now so familiar with—part of the white plains that descend from the before-mentioned snow range I had seen from the slopes of Mount St. Elias from a height of 7000 feet, now stretched out full in view, dazzling, spotless, and immense. Further to the

Cape St. Elias.

west lay Cape Martin, the extremity of a range slightly higher than that of Cape Suckling, and apparently not so hemmed in and closely pressed upon from behind by the seas of ice, which here retire farther inland.

The sun was oppressive. We were rolling lazily in the swell, and close to the Sea-Otter Rocks, where nets are laid during the winter for the otters by the traders. Kaiak Island runs seaward a length of twenty miles; it is flat and thickly forested. At the south end Cape St. Elias, a vast rock apparently 2000 feet high, with rounded outline, rises suddenly, isolated, and with precipitous sides white and shining—a wonderful and unmistakable landmark, with a cloud generally reposing on its top.

Cape St. Elias was named and described by Cook and the early Russian navigators and fur-hunters. The former named the island after Dr. Kaye, and its name seems to have degenerated into Kayak or Kaiak. He also left a bottle with some coins on a wooded eminence not far from the shore, on the east side of the island.

CHAPTER VII.

Arrival at Kaiak—I become a Naval Officer—Hauling in Dog-Fish—The Hunter's Home and the Indian Village—The Tame Bear—Two Norwegians on Cape Suckling—How the Bear came for them—The Habits of the Sea-Otter—Visiting the Indian Hovels—I become an Admiral, and the Chief is presented to me—The Weather changes.

KAIAK ISLAND, *August* 14*th*
(near the Copper River).

THE little schooner seemed in no hurry to be laid up for the winter, for that was to be her fate. Though within a couple of miles of Kaiak we still lay becalmed or nearly so, till at mid-day a boat shot out from the point, behind which the small "store" is situated, containing the three other white inhabitants, all Scandinavians. One of them was Nils' wife, a stout, pleasant, homely, Swedish woman. I soon made their acquaintance, or rather was introduced to them by Nils Andersen. Had I some kind of uniform I could wear? I was to parade as an officer from a man-of-war—the one thing that keeps the Indians in awe. Among the few trade articles calculated to take the Indians' fancy that remained was a gold-

braided cap and military coat with brass buttons, exactly suitable, and fitting to a nicety.

"We were telling the Indians," said Olaf, who was one of the three in the boat, "that the war-ship was coming, and would punish them if they didn't behave themselves. They wanted their

K

big canoe to go to Oodiak, but they will let us have it now to take us to Nuchuk. The bucks left this morning for a four days' hunting-trip. The squaws may clear out when they see the cap with the gold band, and are told that you come from the big war-ship."

At the point the tide was running strongly, and the anchor had to be dropped somewhat suddenly. While the Swedes were conveying the things ashore, I procured a large hook from the cabin, baited it with a piece of salt salmon, tied on a bit of iron as a sinker, attached a line, and allowed it to sink till it touched bottom. My dream was to engage in a struggle with an enormous 400 lb. Alaskan halibut, to wrestle with the great *chavicha* or the king salmon, or to shoot the emperor goose and the sea-lion. I knew there would be no fresh fish ashore, for the Alaskan will never trouble to angle for fresh cod while salted salmon remains in his fish barrel, nor do the traders eat it until winter, when nothing else can be had. As soon as the weight touched bottom, at three fathoms, there came a pull. Hauling in I found the hook broken. A new hook and another bite, and I hauled in a large dog-fish; and without changing the bait, another. Then three more of these " terrors of the ocean " in as many minutes. Clearly dog-fish swarm, and my halibut still remains an experience for the next fine day.

Coming ashore, I found the natives evidently not deeply impressed by the presence in their midst of a naval officer; the two decrepit men, the slovenly squaws, and half naked children did not "clear out," but merely pointed and whispered.

Kaiak.

The settlement of Kaiak is picturesquely situated behind cliffs, facing the mainland, sheltered by the two islands Kaiak and Mitchell. A few Indian hovels, for they are nothing else, are built above high-water mark, and a stairway behind leads to two log houses and the store. A house thatched with bark contains the nets and canoes. A whaleboat and two smaller boats lie hauled up on the beach, painted blue—one light and strong, built in Japan, and subsequently brought over by a schooner to Belkoffsky, one of the most important of the Alaskan settlements of the sea-otter hunters. The store is dark, small, but well supplied. The living-house is so confined that two large bear robes cover half of the entire floor—one of them black, the other a tawny grey, reminding one of the Polar species. Small and few as are the houses of this temporary summer settlement—for the Indians spend the winter on the mainland—the dogs in number and wolfishness "discount" the Yakatat Indian dogs. When not "vexing the doleful ear of night" by concerted howlings together, one or two would surely be "baying the moon." In endeavouring to kill and devour any one of their number who is wounded or off his guard, they equal the celebrated dogs of Constantinople. This canine onslaught upon the weak ones of their number occurs constantly, until (for the dogs have a certain value for hunting purposes) the squaws in a slow and deliberate manner toss large stones which fall with a dull thud among the mass of struggling dogs, "both mongrel, puppy, whelp, and hound, and curs of low degree." But though the foul canine mob thus engages in domestic quarrels and internal dissensions, they band together, acting on the rule of "union is strength," and "bunch up," to use a western phrase, when in self-protection the traders hie on their four large dogs against them. At other times the squaws and children engage in an occupation favourite with monkeys, and search each other's hair for a small insect not unknown to civilisation.

KAIAK ISLAND, *August 16th.*

Opposite the store a young bear occupies a box nailed halfway up a tree. His chief enemy is a spotted dog, which is in the habit of pulling him out of his box by his rope, till he succumbs and falls to earth, bristling with teeth and claws, unless, however, he has been enabled to obtain "purchase" round a branch. But the most agonising moment is when, after a rest, the young bear endeavours to regain the perch from which he has been so rudely pulled. He struggles frantically up the trunk, his claws reach within an inch of the edge of his box, when the spotted dog, springing up an incredible height, brings Bruin by his hind paws again to earth. One of the few errors

Mr. Ivan Petroff has made in his description of Alaska (tenth U.S. Census) is the statement that black bears are found on Kaiak Island. This one broke loose last week, and is the solitary representative of his species here.

The only four-footed animals found on Kaiak are foxes, but these are variously coloured as usual, black, grey, grizzled, and red.

Last night we had some music. A "fair wind" had got up and howled without. An oil lamp lit up the rough hewn beams, the rude furniture strewed with rare skins, nets, guns, and implements, and the healthy bearded faces of the Scandinavian hunters, now English-speaking American citizens. Flute, violin and guitar, with a song appropriately named "The Old Log Cabin," and "Coming up the Golden Stairs." This morning, while the men were away laying up the schooner, I was startled by shouts, and looking out saw Mrs. Nils running to the sea with a bucket. The house had been set on fire by the stove pipe, but was put out after a scare.

KAIAK ISLAND, *August* 17*th*.

Two other Scandinavians arrived last month. They were Norwegians this time, and have built a little log cabin on Point Suckling just opposite.

But they have made a mistake, for the surf renders the landing difficult. They are here now, and cannot get back; and when they succeed in doing so, they may not be able to get off again for weeks. Near them lie large lagoons which fill and empty with the tide, and beyond the lagoons the plains of ice. A week ago one of them shot a sea-otter from the rocks and swam out to bring it ashore, but was obliged to abandon it to save himself from being sucked down by the surf. They have done no "hunting" yet, having been engaged in building their winter quarters. Some two weeks ago they saw a bear three hundred yards away, and both opened on him with 45 cal. Winchesters. Bruin instantly turned and came for them like an express train. By the time the seventh shot was fired, which fortunately proved fatal, the brute was but thirty yards distant. These two Norwegians, like the rest, have succeeded in almost completely throwing off their nationality, even in the spelling of their names. They never speak even to each other in their native tongue, always in English— I beg pardon, in American. Even Mrs. Nils makes heroic struggles. I thought at first it was from a sense of politeness to myself; but no, they have become citizens of the Great Republic, and together with all allegiance to Oscar II. they must discard their native language.

It has rained incessantly, and the one subject that comes uppermost is sea-otters. Nils spoke about them as follows :—

We look at our nets every day the weather will allow us during the winter. Sometimes it is too rough to row the whale boat, and we have to sail her. The skin of an otter taken in the otter nets will last without spoiling from three to five days, if we can't get out to the rocks sooner. After that the sea-worms get at them, and drill holes in them. If the worms did not get at them they would last seven or eight days, for the sea is cold in winter, and helps to keep them fresh. There is a saying that you cannot spoil a sea-otter's skin, do what you will with it. The dead and rotting ones thrown up by the sea can be patched together. Holes in the skin matter nothing—they can be filled up. When two otters get caught in the same net, if they can reach each other they always fight. We have found two dead otters together, and the mouth, nose, and whole face of one of them bitten away. The animal has terrible teeth. One can't approach an otter in the nets till it has been knocked on the head. They are so strong that they frequently carry nets, leads and all, to the surface of the water with them, to breathe; but if two are caught, one impedes the other, and both die from drowning if not from fighting. The nets leave no mark on the skin; they are generally taken with one or both paws through the meshes.

I have taken a *chavicha* or king salmon and a sea-otter out of the same net. On one memorable occasion we took seven otters out of one net and four out of another. One man near Belkoffsky took twenty-four out of one net one night after a gale. The Indians usually only hunt land fur in winter, not sea-otters, for the sea is too rough for canoes. They always use bows and arrows for sea-otters, and will only use a gun when they are close and cannot miss. They have an idea that guns frighten away the otters; or perhaps loading takes too much time, for they use muzzle-loaders. In winter the otters are driven by the gales to take refuge near shore, in lee of the islands; but in summer they can only be found out at sea.

My brother and my wife's brother are coming out this winter, and will build a house on that point of Little Kaiak you see just opposite. They are not sailors, so I had no use for them this summer. This winter I shall lend them nets and let them try what they can make of it. They will work the nets at some rocks beyond the point over there.

We were three years, continued Nils, sea-otter hunting on the Island of Gusina, further west, near Belkoffsky. But there are so many white men that we determined to move. Besides, the Alaska Company sends fleets of Indians with their "bidarkies" there every summer to hunt sea-otters. When a sea-otter dives you can never tell where it will come up next. It can remain below for over twenty minutes without coming to the surface to breathe.

We pay from forty to sixty dollars each for the skins to the Indians. They are used for trimming, and would be too expensive to make whole coats of. They practically last for ever. The otters don't feed on fish; we hardly ever find fish inside them when we cut them up—generally sea-slugs and sea-urchins; a favourite food is cuttle-fish.

One day we saw an otter, but had no rifle with us in the boat. We rowed towards it, however, as a matter of course, and found a large cuttle-fish clinging to its head, and we were able to kill the otter with an oar. Bits of the arms of this *octopus* were in the otter's stomach. Its arms were three feet long. Seals are often killed in this way, but no one we have seen had ever heard of a sea-otter taken thus.

Fur-seal skins are best dyed in London. The secret has never been found out. Some one from San Francisco once got employment as a workman by the London firm for two years, but he knew no more about their secret at the end of the two years than when he began. The dyeing is the mystery. The long hairs can be plucked out in 'Frisco as well as they can be in London, but the dye will not last. Here are two fur caps, one of London dyed seal-skin, that I bought last year at Bremen when I went home to Sweden to fetch my wife—it cost three pounds ten; and here (showing me a lighter coloured one) is a San Francisco seal-skin cap that only cost half that price. I have worn it a good deal, yet you can see that it never was as good as the London one.

The trees? Yes, the trees are grown and bent into a fixed position by the continual winds from the north-east. We get very strong east winds here. West of this, towards Kodiak, they get more west wind. It mostly blows from the west

there in winter. I have noticed that if it blows
north-east without rain for a few hours, then it is
sure to last; but if we have a north-easter with
rain from the first, it is soon over. The east wind
always brings rain, and the wind is mostly east
at Kaiak. A falling glass in summer often means
calms here. The glass generally rises for east
winds and rain.

Kaiak Island, *August* 18*th*.

I went round the Indian houses to-day. At
Yakatat there were six houses, each forty feet
square and fifteen in height, accommodating several
families. In front of each house was a platform
from which one entered the building by a small
round door, requiring some considerable squeezing
to accomplish. By a flight of steps one descended
to the floor, which was strewn with gravel, and sunk
to increase the space inside. In the very centre
was the fireplace, from which the smoke ascended
through a large square hole in the roof. Round
three sides ran a broad seat, on which one stepped
to enter the low, draughty, sleeping-place behind.
Four large wooden idols graced the chief's house,
like "totem poles," carved in the usual style. The
Kaiak houses were differently constructed. After
much constriction one manages to insinuate oneself

into a windy hovel barely five feet high. It is necessary to keep crouching to avoid the shelves full of dried salmon skins. The children commence crying, and the dogs growl and retreat into corners, but the grown members of the family preserve a stolid apathy. Small round holes eighteen inches

Indian Hovels at Kaiak.

in diameter lead to the sleeping places, built out from the main walls.

Among the numerous nasty customs, that of all ages and both sexes using the same quid of tobacco, promiscuously, it being rolled up in a ball with ashes and kept in a small box or bag, strikes one as the most repugnant.

The party of Indian sea-otter hunters, composed

of twenty-four men and twelve "bidarkies" or sealskin canoes, returned this afternoon from Cape St. Elias with two otters. As soon as they were seen coming, a pair of old Swedish naval epaulets was rummaged up and fastened on my coat, till I resembled an exhibition of gold lace or caricature of an admiral in full dress. I protested it was overdoing the thing. But no—I must come down and have the chief presented to me as soon as he had landed. His name was Klok-Shegees. In the evening the medicine-man was summoned, and I had to pretend to be taking notes. I did actually take down the names of those present, such as Cronook, Tookh, Yaak, Schlateet Katay, Stagaat, Katata, Kokoonook, and Ke, and the *shawaan* himself, Doushagow. He would take us himself to Nuchuk in his yak or large canoe, with two others to paddle, for three blankets, and we are to start when the weather becomes fine.

Every day the natives have been gathering cockles at low water. The "tongues" of these they were now salting and smoking. In one hut an aged woman never for one instant ceased groaning loudly and depressingly. In another a man was dying of consumption; some women were rubbing his body with their hands moistened with saliva.

Klok-Shegees in his "Store" Clothing.

These Indians, like the Chukche Esquimaux, do not expectorate on the gravel floor. Whatever the

reason may be, it has nothing to do with delicacy; but unlike the Chukche dogs, these dogs *can* bark. Doushagow, the *shawaan*, who is to take us to Nuchuk, has voluntarily cut his long hair; perhaps because it is more civilised, or possibly in consequence of having heard of the *shawaan* at Kilisnoo, in South-east Alaska, who for certain misdeeds had his head shaved and *painted red* on board *The Pinta*.

KAIAK ISLAND, *August* 19*th*.

For the last five days it has rained without a moment's interval. Wind moderate from the northeast. To-day the wind is south-west, and consequently it is beautifully fine. This change in the direction of the wind is invariably followed by a corresponding change in the weather. This rule holds good from the St. Elias Alps to the Kenai Peninsula, if not farther. We are preparing to start to-morrow, as the *shawaan* thinks the swell too heavy to-day, though where or how it could harm us is at present wrapped in obscurity, for none of the white men have travelled by canoe to Nuchuk, and though Nils and Olaf speak the language fairly, an Indian is quite incapable of entering into any explanations. The Indian jargon here consists of a mixture of Chilcat, Russian, and Chinook.

These Indians designate themselves as Chilcats, as though connected with the Chilcats and Chilcoots at the head of Lynn's Canal, but are known to these traders as Coloshes. The traders have arranged that the medicine-man is to take us to Nuchuk for fifteen dollars, or as before-mentioned for three blankets. He has bargained to bring his wife with him, who will paddle, and also two other Indians.

CHAPTER VIII.

We are forced to stop at Martin Point—Raw Salmons' Noses—A Bear shot—A Drunken Indian Village—Sliding over the Mud of the Copper River Delta—The Squaw kills a Salmon—Camp on an Island—Estuary of the Copper River—Camp on Hawkins Islands—The Indians Washing—Caught in a Gale—Salmon-fishing Extraordinary—Description of an Alaskan Scene—Captain Cook in Prince William Sound—We arrive at Nuchuk.

CAMP AT THE INDIAN VILLAGE, POINT MARTIN,
August 20*th*, 8 P.M.

WE paddled from the beach at Kaiak at 10 A.M. this morning, amid salvoes of guns from the Indians, to which we replied from the canoe. Having made the fifteen miles to this place in four hours across Controller's Bay, as Cook named it, we endeavoured feebly to induce the *shawaan* to continue until nightfall, as, though at present landing was easy, any increase in the wind might raise a swell, that would keep us prisoners for days, the only protection being two small islands. Yet the old man insisted that we must stay at the Indian village here, though it was but two o'clock in the afternoon.

A crowd of Indians came out, one stationed on high ground, whence he could see the breakers coming, and choose a calm moment for us to shoot into shore, where the rest soon hauled us high and dry upon the beach.

If we were in the estuary of the Copper River, behind the sand-bars, we should be independent of

At Martin Point.

the weather. To-day is fine, the opening into the lagoons is close at hand—to-morrow may be stormy—yet we are compelled to lie all the day idle.

We cooked some salmon for dinner on the beach, the *shawaan* having previously sliced off raw, with a knife, and eaten the whole skin of the heads and the bridges of the noses of the fish.

The Indian village is partially fenced with stockading; the houses are merely single-roomed, but of moderate size. Long ago, there was a fur-trading post here, but it was abandoned. From this neighbourhood, northwards to Cook's Inlet, white mountain goats are found on the mountains.

We were now on the mainland, and as the day was fine, I set out with the rifle to look for anything in the shape of game that might chance along the shore to the eastward. Some miles off a small stream emptied into the sea. Fresh tracks of bear were to be seen along the bank, and I was soon fortunate enough to find one of these animals engaged in searching for fish apparently, as he was crouching on a rock, occasionally dipping a paw in the water, and not yet aware of any danger. Stalking the animal with care to within a distance of fifty yards, I aimed carefully from behind a tree at the shoulder low down, and planted an English express solid bullet in a vital place, for he fell into the stream, and scrambling on to the opposite shore, lay down *in extremis*. I remained concealed till sure that he was powerless to do any damage. A second shot was unnecessary. The animal was of moderate size, but the fur was poor and thin, as might have been expected. The winter coat is the thickest, and the skins are then more valuable. It was not worth the trouble of skinning; some of the Indians will go for it to-morrow if they want it.

This evening in the tent the *shawaan* endeavoured to explain, in a mixture of English and Chinook words, that he wished to be, or was, *shawaan* of all the Chilcats—would I give him a paper? He was promised one when we reached Nuchuk. Could I draw a picture of San Francisco? I replied it was too large. Was it larger than this village? I took up a grain of sand and said "Point Martin;" then a whole handful, and said "San Francisco." He then said he would paddle us well to Nuchuk if I would only give him a paper to say he was "goot shawaan," if the man-of-war came. Yes, to-morrow it would be fine, and we would start early.

Camp on an Island,
Mouth of the Copper River,
August 21st, 5 p.m.

The *shawaan* and his wife came back from the village this morning long after the sun had risen and lay down in a drunken sleep, blear-eyed and disfigured by their debauch. To rouse them we had to take their tent down from over their heads. Luckily the weather is fine, and the surf has moderated. They insisted on boiling some salmon before starting, and asked us to hire two more Indians to paddle. It was thought best to acquiesce, to avoid further delay. Meanwhile the natives came down to the beach, all being drunk, and we experienced a *mauvais quart d'heure*, but fortunately they were amiably drunk. Our men were sobered by wading through the surf when we launched. The only way of getting off without delay was to carry the canoe ourselves to the water's edge, which we did, and got away at 8 A.M. The inhabitants had been holding a "pot-latch" the whole night on the vile stuff they distil from sugar, for which purpose there are retorts in nearly every house here.

When an Indian or Indians have to do anything, one can never be sure beforehand concerning any particular portion of the proceedings. We were not, it now appeared, going to cross the bar of the Copper River at all, though the swell was quite moderate. A mile away the Indians turned shorewards and beached the canoe. Everything was carried over the sand ridge. We found ourselves at the commencement or extreme corner of the tidal lagoons of the Copper River delta. The tide was out, and nothing but wet mud was to be seen lying between steep timbered slopes and the sand ridge. It was ten o'clock by the time the canoe was lying on the mud loaded, and everything ready for a new start. Then commenced a, to me, novel method of locomotion, viz., sliding over mud with the canoe, like sledging on snow.

The yak, though thirty feet in length and five in breadth, was hewn out of a single tree; her bottom was smooth and keelless, and glided swiftly and easily over the black, slippery ooze, which gave out a disagreeable and putrefying smell. We slipped about on it with our bare feet as we pushed behind the canoe to meet the tide which was now flowing.

Doushagow's (the medicine-man's) wife now came up with a fine salmon she had killed in one of the small brooks that issued from the forest; and, reaching a channel of running water, we were able to float the canoe. As the tide rose the channels seemed to abound with salmon, which kept leaping out of water, whichever side one turned to look. Meanwhile the two Point Martin Indians had been paid, had accepted the agreed amount, and had left us.

We were now opposite the first opening from the bar through the sand reefs into the Copper River delta. The whole delta now opened out to view, bounded on both sides by ranges of snow-capped mountains, which unfolded gradually to view as we neared the centre of the expanse, an area of at least thirty miles each way. On a point were two Indian houses, where we waited for the tide to rise. Two canoes meantime came up across the flat. When they reached any stretch of bare mud, the men would paddle on as though it were water, and the light "battok" would "snake" over the slippery surface like a fish struggling to regain its native element. In one of the canoes lay a seal freshly killed.

We camped for the night on a small island a third of the way across—bare, but strewn with dry driftwood suitable for a fire.

CAMP IN A COVE, HAWKINS ISLANDS,
August 22d, 10 P.M.

This morning I woke at 3.15 A.M., and roused Doushagow, for the tide was covering the mud rapidly. It was blowing bitterly cold from the glaciers, but it was a north-westerly or fine-weather wind. He wore his coat of bird-skins with the feather side turned inwards. The two other Indians were as usual lightly clad in cotton cloth, and shivering from the chilliness of the air.

Being now towards the centre of the estuary of the river, the mountain scenery of the shores lay spread in panoramic view, commencing from Martin Point, the east extremity, to Cape Whit-

August 22d, 5 A.M., looking N.W.

shed on the west. While looking northward the eye plunges into the narrowing valley from which the Copper River issues, until barred by a blue range of mountains fifty miles distant which impedes further view. From Point Martin to where the mountains first commence to close or approach together, shutting in the river between them, a distance of twenty miles, a low dark range stretches, from three to four thousand feet in height, on which I counted eighteen small glaciers on the summits and four large glaciers in the valleys below. This line of mountains is broken midway by a gap eight miles wide, which allows a view of an extensive snowy range lying behind, the highest summit of which appears to be at least thirteen or fourteen thousand feet in height, with six other peaks of slightly lesser altitude near it.

A Man of Oodiak; sketched at Nuchuk, Oct. 9th.

The opposite shore of the delta is of much more remarkable formation. From the valley from which the river issues to the middle portion of this shore the mountains project out into the tidal alluvial plain. On this part I counted fifteen small summit glaciers and two large valley glaciers, spreading out, like all Alaskan glaciers, with beautiful fan-like shape to the river level. But from this projecting point to Cape Whitshed, twenty-five miles to the west, the shores trend back and form a deep wide bay, in which are situated the two villages of Alagnuk and Oodiak. This portion of the mountains is thickly timbered below, and almost devoid of summit glaciers, except a few very small ones. But there are three large valley glaciers to be seen—one a double glacier. Behind and back lie a lofty sea of peaks. Two close by are *aiguilles*, sharp and cone-shaped.

August 22d, 1 P.M.

Another, which seems the highest, rises in castellated terraces to a height of apparently 12,000 feet.

At 6.30 A.M., the wind, which had favoured us, died quite away. At 9.30 we were stopped by shallows while endeavouring to find a channel. The bottom now being sandy, it was no longer feasible to push the canoe over the bare flats. I shot three ducks which came alongside within a few yards with a rifle, my gun being left with the *New York Times* party.

We wished to stay quiet until the tide rose sufficiently to allow us to proceed, but Doushagow insisted on returning by a long detour against tide and river current to one of the bare flat islands, where the Indians could find driftwood enough to cook the salmon and ducks for themselves. Putting out again at 1 P.M., with a flowing tide, we kept on steadily until 7 P.M., at times using the sail. The two Indians in the bow kept on paddling whether there was a favourable breeze or no, the *shawaan* steering in the stern, and his wife occasionally paddling a little. We were now at Cape Whitshed, and about to land for the night in a convenient cove; but the breeze springing up strongly from the east, we continued on, and camped by a small brook on this island as the last light vanished in the west.

Another Camp on Hawkins Islands,
Six Miles farther West,
August 23d, 10 P.M.

As soon as the yak was hauled up last night, two of the Indians disappeared, and returned in ten minutes from the direction of the little stream with fifteen salmon, of from three to six pounds' weight. It was evident that one could hardly starve, though the store of pilot bread should run quite out.

About midnight it commenced raining, accompanied by the usual east wind. The tents were sheltered by beetling cliffs and overhanging boughs of trees. It was clear from the decided bent and growing to the westward of the branches of the trees that this was the normal and prevailing direction of the wind, while the damp luxuriant undergrowth proclaimed plainly in unspoken words, "*la pluie, encore la pluie, et toujours la pluie.*"

How the Trees Grow in Alaska.

Any photograph of the forests during a perfect calm would give the idea that a violent easterly wind was raging, the tortured and wind-torn branches having grown and fixed themselves into the position given to them by the strong prevailing winds, stretching their petrified and supplicating arms towards the west.

This morning the Indians were to be seen washing with soap and water, while the only vessel containing the latter was the large saucepan just brought to boil our breakfast of salmon in; it remaining, notwithstanding, perfectly unsullied all the while. This was as mystifying as any conjuring trick, till Doushagow was observed to stoop over the pot and suck up a mouthful, which he squirted over his hands while applying the soap, after the fashion of a Chinaman.

The wind now increased every moment. The Indians advised remaining, and the *shaawan* put on his greatcoat of bear-gut over the one he already wore of bird-skins. Nevertheless we set off, and found the wind more violent than we expected, raising small waves which threatened to engulf the canoe. As we coasted along the shore there was shelter from the ocean swell, yet we shipped some seas. With but a single mast and small sprit-sail in the bows, she flew over the water at a most exciting speed, quite outpacing the steep and curling billows. Olaf, who was holding the sheet-ropes, complained that they were cutting into his hands, every one else keeping their paddles in the water to keep her straight before the wind, while the *shawaan* kept up an incessant shouting of orders to the two other Indians. Presently the sprit bent and cracked, and had to be held together. It was too unsafe to last long, so she was turned into the first inlet, beached and emptied, and once more camp was pitched. In half an hour we had completed six miles, our total for to-day. More beetling cliffs offered dry stowage room and a sheltered spot for the fire. More surprises were yet in store. A small brooklet, but a yard wide and three inches deep, trickled from the woods across the beach. It was completely crowded with salmon, and the water being not of a depth to cover them, their backs were bare. At first sight it seemed that some of the fish were affected with a fungoid growth, but on lifting one from the water it became evident that the white patches were the marks of struggles in the shallow water over the sharp stones and shingle. There appeared to be truly a greater bulk of salmon than there was of water in the brook. As I approached, their wriggling and splashing almost emptied the pools of the little water that existed in them, in efforts to find shelter in the deeper water that did not exist. Some lay still, as though exhausted; others made feeble movements with the tail, while, anywhere in a length of ten yards of the stream, was food enough for us for a week. I followed the brook some twenty yards up its course, until fallen trees and damp bushes turned me back, and everywhere the surface was a mass of the moving and swaying backs of the foolish fish—the lordly salmon in water barely deep enough to harbour a minnow! Some had insinuated themselves into extraordinary and seemingly inaccessible positions, and could neither advance nor retreat without landing themselves high and dry. This explained the ease with which the Indians returned last night loaded with fish. Dead salmon, half eaten by foxes, lay strewn along the banks. Tea, with boiled salmon and salmon-roe, formed our lunch; boiled salmon and roe, with tea, composed the dinner; and tea, with boiled salmon-roe and salmon, the supper; and still the east wind blows and the rain descends. At their meals the Indians generally commence with tea and a small piece of "hard-tack," and then eat the skins of the raw salmons' heads before attacking the contents of the pot of boiled salmon.

The stream was gradually rising. From the tent door, through the smoke and rain, I watched the salmon ascending the streamlet in Indian file, fish succeeding and following fish in endless procession; each fish resembling a miniature screw-steamer unballasted, with the propeller half out of water and splashing, as they ploughed up the shallows like moving fountains. In fact, the sight from the brook-side was as of a vast fishmonger's slab, as there averaged twelve salmon to every two square yards of water. Some had been edged and pressed on to dry land by the very crowds of their companions, and were shuffling over the beach to regain their native element.

Meanwhile the Indians had built an enormous fire, which was raising clouds of steam from everything. The rain was falling with Alaskan earnestness, in columns and sheets of heavy drops, which even splashed in dew-like spray through the material of the tents, until we pinned our mackintoshes on the outside.

NUCHUK, INDIAN VILLAGE, HINCHINBROOK ISLAND,
PRINCE WILLIAM SOUND, *August 26th.*

It was the last effort of the east wind, for at midnight the wind became westerly, bringing with it, as a matter of course, fine weather and a clear sky, and 6 A.M. saw us once more *en route.*

We were now passing down the straits between the islands of Hawkins and Hinchinbrook, as the early navigators called them. The shores were thickly wooded, with steep cliffs and innumerable little bays, while small islands were distributed here and there. The narrowest part of the channel is but a hundred yards in width, with two rocky islands in the opening. The stillness and dim light of early morning lent a charm to the scenery, which was now Alaskan at its very best, in form, in colour, and surroundings; the high-prowed canoe with a suspicion of a Venetian gondola lurking somewhere about its front, or embodied in its black paint; the couple of black-haired Indians, brown and lithe, paddling in front monotonously; the dark green water, profoundly deep; the steep purple cliffs, furrowed by the waves, indented with small bays, coves, and caves, and shadowed by overhanging firs and shrubs; the snow-patched hills of Nuchuk, resembling the Snowdon range, and reddened by the rising sun; the bird life, and the lines of kelp or bladder weed fringing the shore, along deep water, and in which now and again a silver salmon would leap and splash. Nor must I omit from the catalogue of sensations the peculiar faint indescribable Indian odour that pervaded the canoe, with a flavour and a rich raciness all its own—an odour which, if it could be once more inhaled, were I in any part of the world, would revive the most vivid memory of Alaska.

Next moment we shot round the north-west cape of Nuchuk, to find Prince William Sound spread before us, dotted with large islands, the tops of which seemed to quiver and float in the mirage. The sharp white ice-peaks fringing the greater part of the horizon were of smaller mould than the gigantic masses of the St. Elias range; but powdered with fresh snow, and in the absence of any such competitors, they formed a sufficiently attractive background to one of the most interesting inland seas or *fjords* on the coast of Alaska. Commencing from the mountains of the mysterious Kenai Peninsula, which are low, with broad flat glaciers, as the eye sweeps round, the ranges gradually increase in height, till they attain their loftiest elevation in a bold ridge embosomed in extensive fields of snow near the actual head of the Sound.

Vancouver's boats explored portions of Prince William Sound. On their landing at what they named Port Gravina, near the present Indian village of Tatcekluk, they found "an old bear nearly at the top of a pine-tree with two cubs; the former immediately descended and made its escape, but the young ones were shot, and afforded an excellent dinner." The party, however, had fared tolerably well on this expedition, having shot many wild fowl, and on most of the rocks where they had landed eggs had been procured in great abundance (June 1794).

We now turned to the south for Port Etches. Promontory and headland succeeded one another as we skirted the northern shore of the island. For some reason the Indians had cooked no breakfast for themselves before setting out, nor did they break their fast until we rounded the last point and came in view of Nuchuk village—seven hours steady going from the start; for an Indian can eat much or little according to circumstances, or at short or long intervals indifferently, or go without food altogether, and yet be happy.

A store and fur-agency, the houses having been built by the Russians, a small church, and fifteen to twenty Indian or Aleut houses, situated on a peninsula jutting out into a noble bay, and forming one of the best harbours in Alaska—such, in few words, is Port Etches or Nuchuk, which is the only evidence of civilisation in the district.

As we sailed down towards the settlement, for a fair wind had sprung up, we could see the inhabitants running down to the shore. The surf was quiet enough to allow our landing on the outer beach instead of having to make the long round of the promontory into the inner harbour, and as soon as we arrived the fur agent offered us the use of his house.

CHAPTER IX.

Our Life at Nuchuk—A Native Ball—The Natives start on a Sea-Otter Hunt in Bidarkies—Description of a Bidarky—Climbing after Grouse—Millions of Salmon—Spearing and Hooking them—Salmon-Drying—Our Russian Bath—A Description of Nuchuk and the Game and Food of Prince William Sound—How the Natives Live, and how the Alaska Commercial Company of San Francisco Trades with them—The Natives as Captain Cook found them.

> "Where in the still deep water,
> Sheltered from waves and blasts,
> Bristles the dusky forest
> Of Byrsa's thousand masts,
> Where fur-clad hunters wander
> Amidst the northern ice."

NUCHUK, *September 2d*, 1886.

ON the four evenings following our arrival "dances" were held, as the whole male population was daily in expectation of leaving on a fortnight's sea-otter hunt—dependent on the weather.

The first night's entertainment was in the house of Vanya, brother of the second chief. The next in that of Pavil, the Tyoon, or chief. Then Peter, the Shekaizik, or second chief, was the host.

But when we had again to dance until two in the morning in the small, close, single room of the

WE BECOME DISSIPATED. 183

Tyoon, which was his house, or give mortal offence, it was with reluctant steps that we led our Indian brides, or rather partners, along the garbage-strewn pathway, preceded by players on the accordion and the guitar, to where bright oil lamps and an unusual number of candles marked his abode. It was in just and merited retaliation, for, the first night, when the second chief had been honoured, it was the Tyoon who had cleared his room and removed his stove and his door in expectation of our arrival. A description of one night's festivity will serve for all four.

Nuchuk—The Baidars or Baiderars of the Copper River Indians.

Imagine, then, a one-roomed log-house, every corner and seat occupied with children and grown persons dressed in their dirty prints or cotton shirts. The infants sleep peaceably through the noise on a bed under which some tamed wild-duck live and feed. The half-dozen Aleut squaws who know the figures of the Russian quadrille occupy prominent places on the floor, unless they have accompanied us from the trader's house. "Partners" is called, and we make sides and perform the different figures to the various words of command shouted in a monotone by the trader, and which soon became mechanically familiar, such as "sides forward and back, one lady over," or "balance and swing—swing," or "grand right and left with double

Noshek — the Russian Church.

swing," which invariably ended in confused collisions, for the frame of the Aleut squaw is none of the most fragile. Keeping on one's hat, smoking, or expectorating on the floor, would of course be quite in order. About midnight tea and pilot-bread appears; after the men are satisfied, then the cups are filled again for "the ladies."

After the quadrille, an Aleut dance by two of the men takes place, which so shakes the house, that were the structure not of wood, one would fear for its safety, so energetic are their leaps and bounds. Then a waltz—only room for one couple, who aim to revolve as rapidly and as long as possible, till dizzy and exhausted, they sink down on some unoccupied part of the floor. Such is an Alaskan ball.

On the 30th the men all left on a sea-otter hunt

Bidarkies.

in seventeen bidarkies. The boats having been laid in a row on the beach, and everything prepared, they filed away in procession to their small Russian church for a blessing. The priest is the trader's cook. After this ceremony they must not enter any house, but quickly launch and away without further ado.

These bidarkies are constructed of sealskin over a light wooden frame. No nail is used, as that would be considered unlucky. Consequently the parts are bound together with roots and sinews, and over all is sewed the skin or *luftak*. The curiously shaped double prow the Indians will never vary in shape.

On the deck are two (rarely one, though sometimes three) round holes, to admit of the occupants kneeling. A considerable amount can be carried, distributed in small packages in the interior. Thus the trader lately returned from the mainland with thirty-seven "red salmon," besides bedding and utensils; while to-day an Indian arrived carrying in his "one-hatch" bidarky the greater part of a bear, some ducks, a heron, and some "silver salmon." There being no room to use any bailer, an egg-shaped tube is taken to suck up any water that might have entered. It is affirmed by whites and Indians to be the safest of any of the smaller craft in rough weather.

Invariably with these boats is used a waterproof coat, or *Kamleyga* of bear guts sewn together, or sea-lion guts; this is tied round the circular opening in such a manner that no water can, by any possibility short of leakage, reach the interior of the canoe. When once launched, the natives will pass through breaking surf in a bidarky, under which she appears to dive like a duck or loom, and will face weather unsafe for an ordinary canoe.

To launch their "two-hatch" bidarkies, the bow or forward paddler first took his seat, the boats being at the water's edge. Watching his opportunity the other then pushed her off, and jumped not in but *on* her, till he could shake the water from his legs, both paddling their best in the meantime till beyond the breakers.

I ascended the hill yesterday, on the west side of the bay, on the second attempt, being repulsed the first time by the thickness of the underbrush. On the far horizon, fifty miles south, was visible Middleton Island, where a small settlement has been established. The Company propose to start a ranche of foxes there. The best farming land in Alaska is situated on the island, which is not great praise. Hitherto the only crop has been one of the eggs of sea-fowls, which breed there in incredible numbers. There is no harbour. An Indian carried my trade gun, for ptarmigan abound, and I found a covey on the ridge.

The view of Prince William Sound was but slightly more extensive than from below, but the view over Nuchuk Island was worth the trouble of the ascent. Coming down another way in pursuit of a flock of ptarmigan some smooth and difficult grass slopes had to be descended, at an angle of quite sixty degrees from the horizontal. The Indian advised taking off boots, for some of the nails had come out; meanwhile one had to slide down the very steepest of grassy gullies with "five points of contact," assisted by the bushes and ruggedness of the slope.

NUCHUK, *September* 4*th*, 1886.

Yesterday I went in the "dory" to the nearest river to observe the salmon. Before starting there was quite an excitement at what appeared to be the schooner; the telescope resolved the object into a floating tree with branches standing out like masts.

Reaching the river, the water seemed alive with the *karbusha* or hogback salmon. It was nowhere over a foot and a half in depth. Long processions of salmon swam up and down the stream, those descending keeping mostly next the banks. None showed any alarm at the boat, and when our craft had become half filled with struggling fish the novelty of spearing them had partly worn off.

The Alaskan salmon in fresh water (I had disproved this theory as to salt water at Sitka), is said to care nothing for any artificial bait. Throwing out from the boat across the current a spoon-bait tied to a line and weighted, for the rod had long since been lost on the shores of Icy Bay, I drew it slowly in. For fear of hooking foul of one out of the dense crowd of salmon, it was necessary not to throw more than a yard or two from the boat. Most of the fish were spent and seemed sluggish and tame; but one or two, and these always clean fresh-run fish, would summon energy for a feeble rush, and if it were not dragged through the water too rapidly would open wide their jaws and close them upon the piece of glittering metal —all this in full view close alongside the boat.

Next, a large halibut hook was tied on the line, and cast across the stream; the whole length of line could then be felt, borne up and prevented from sinking by the mass of moving backs on which it rested, and when it was drawn in, the point of the hook usually found out some holding spot on some part of a salmon, which could be dragged splashing and struggling into the now loaded boat.

On the way back we fired several rifle shots at a moving object quite like a sea-otter, before making the discovery that it was an *Indian dog* swimming at least a fourth of a mile from shore. The impingement of the bullets seemed to add fresh vigour to its movements.

Nothing can be imagined in fish nomenclature more confusing than the varying names of Alaskan salmon. On this portion of the coast they are catalogued into six kinds, as follows :—

First, the *chavicha* or "king" salmon, which runs or enters the rivers from May 20th till August, being most plentiful in June. In Cook's Inlet their proportion at this time to the other salmon is as one to three. The greatest length of the king salmon is six feet, and weight 100 lbs. At the two canning and salting works in Cook's Inlet 15,500 were taken in 1880. In addition to the Kassiloff and Kenai Rivers in Cook's Inlet, the king salmon is also found in the Alanuk or Aleganuk River, near the Indian village of that name at the mouth of the Copper River; brought from which river to this place a fresh king salmon is worth just ten cents.

Second, the "red" salmon or *krasnee*, which runs the whole summer. These two kinds of salmon are the only sorts used for canning, except at Kassiloff, where the silver salmon is also used.

The nearest river from Nuchuk for red salmon is the *Isha* in Prince William Sound, where are ruins of old Russian or Indian weirs, though a few may be found in almost any river.

Third, the "silver" salmon or *kiswich*, of a whiter tinge of flesh.

Fourth, the "steelhead" or *somga*, which resembles the silver salmon, except in possessing a head invulnerable to blows.

Fifth, comes the "hogback" or *karbusha*, which runs in August and September.

Sixth, the "dog" salmon or *hiko*, running at the same time—a coarse fish, with large teeth and scales.

The women are now engaged in splitting salmon for drying for their winter supply of *eukola* or *ookla*, contenting themselves with the hogback salmon and sea-trout at present, as the silver salmon has not yet arrived in the rivers of the bay. The value here of a salmon dried and smoked for keeping is just one cent. A portion only of the salmon is taken—a thin layer adhering to the skin, and another to the backbone—for a greater thickness would take longer to dry. The supply of salmon is practically unlimited.

Every Saturday we use the small Russian bath which is built on to one side of the old store-house. It consists of two small apartments with thick log walls. In the inner room is a fireplace without any chimney for heating to redness the pile of rocks placed upon it. It takes about five hours to accomplish this; then the fire is extinguished, the window is closed, a vessel of cold and another of hot water are placed within, and the bath is ready. One by one we four white men take our baths, and afterwards the Indian girls and women employed about the house. One has to be cautious not to touch the ceiling, begrimed as it is with soot. To raise the temperature to any extent required, one has merely to sprinkle water upon the red-hot stones in the corner.

Jaw-bone of a "Dog-salmon." Nuchuk, Aug. 1886.

Between Nuchuk or Hinchinbrook Island and Sukluk or Montague Island is the entrance to Prince William Sound (called Nenoork or Chugak), through which the tidal currents race back and forth with great velocity.

Nuchuk Bay is walled in between two straight

Nuchuk—Our Home for Two Months.

and parallel ranges of steep mountains, on which are some comparatively insignificant glaciers. At the head of the bay is a solitary cone, probably an extinct volcano. A harbour with a narrow entrance is formed by a large island connected with the western cape by a sand ridge. This is subdivided into an inner harbour too shallow for ships by another sand ridge. Where the first sand-bar joins the island is situated the Indian village and the Alaska Company's store of Nuchuk. Captain Cook once anchored in the outer harbour. The trader's house is on the site of the old fort called St. Constantine—now no more. In short, Port Etches or Nuchuk was once a Russian stronghold

Prince William Sound, Alaska, with Nuchuk Harbour.

and a populous Indian settlement, and played an important part in the early history of Alaska.

From hence westward the Aleuts take the place of the Indians, excepting in Cook's Inlet, and Russian traits are often observable. As the mixture of different nationalities is said to produce strong offspring, so this addition of Russian blood has probably prolonged the existence of the Indian races. They seemed a far finer set mentally and physically than the Yakatats. Their ethnographical divisions and a theory of the migrations of the different tribes are set forth in Petroff's U.S. Report on Alaska (1880). Roughly speaking, the mouth of the Copper River is the spot which has been the limit or point of junction of the Indian races which belong to the South, to the North, and to the East.

In January the sea-lions enter the sound, and in May the fur-seals arrive. The latter remain a week or two, occasionally shifting their ground before disappearing until the following year. Whence they come and whither they go is a mystery unknown even to the Indians. Perchance the Fur Seal Islands is their next rendezvous.

a man of Oodiak nuchuk. Oct 9. 86.

In September and October swarms of ducks and geese enter the bays and inlets of the sound. Seven of these wild geese, lately captured by some Indians, are now feeding round the house like the common or domestic goose, being dark brown birds, with a white band on the head. In Prince William Sound any quantity of salmon can be speared or netted the whole summer through, but so improvident are the natives that they have frequently omitted to dry sufficient salmon, or turn it into *eukla*, for the winter's consumption, and have been dependent for food upon the trader. Bears and goats are killed all the year round on the mainland, the latter principally in the winter, when the snow drives them down to the sea-level.

An Alaskan Indian Halibut Hook.

In November the geese have departed south, not to reappear till March, but most of the ducks remain the whole winter. In that month also the last is seen of the salmon, but their place is taken by sea fish—the cod, halibut, and herring. But rarely is the weather calm enough to allow of their capture out of the small canoes. The lines used for sea-fishing are made of dried seaweed, known as kelp or bladder weed, the resort of the sea-otter.

The abundance of the edible berries is marvellous—strawberries, black currants, gooseberries, blueberries, blackberries, salmon-berries, and lastly, in October, the delicious cranberries. Such is the wealth of food lavished upon the indolent native, Creole, Aleut, or Indian, who now lives for the capture of the sea-otter, and sometimes dies for it. The characteristics of these natives are alike from the most remote of the Aleutian Islands on the west to Cape Flattery on the east. As long as they have money in plenty—if they have been successful in their last sea-otter hunt, that is—they will do no work whatever, but will spend it lavishly and improvidently in buying useless articles from the nearest store of the Alaska Commercial Company, such as eau-de-cologne (which they drink), and fashionable boots, which they soon throw away. When the last dollar is gone, they will ask for a loan of provisions, to set out on another hunt or on a trapping expedition.

The system of trading which is carried on by the Alaska Commercial Company, shortly expressed, is as follows. As long as Indians and sea-otters continue to exist it will continue to be a lucrative proceeding, if not overdone, which would surely be the case if there were any competition. Every spring a cargo of suitable articles is shipped from San Francisco to Kodiak and to Unalaska, the two main stores, and thence by schooner distributed to the various fur posts or trading stations from Cook's Inlet to the Aleutian Islands. This trading material consists of cheap articles of clothing, cotton prints, flour, sugar, tobacco, lard, and the usual assortment of articles of that description, besides many others of a most surprising character. As the skins are brought to the trader—sea-otter, fox, bear, wolf, lynx, musk-rat, marten, land-otter, mink, or whatever they may be—a fixed price is paid in silver dollars, which of course are soon paid back into the store for goods.

Cook remarks as a curious fact that the coast Indians could never have traded sea-otter skins to the inland tribes, for these skins were never seen at Hudson's Bay. Yet the natives of Prince William Sound valued the sea-otter skins at that time not so much as those of wild cats and martens, and no more than other skins, for they gladly parted with them for a few beads. He was amused with their "antic gestures," such as standing up motionless in a boat or *baidar* for fifteen minutes quite naked and with arms extended. Their dress then, as it is now, was in *parkas* or coats of ground squirrel skin and of whale gut.

CHAPTER X.

Life with the Indians on the Copper River.

AT Nuchuk I found the diary and the record of the experiences of the only white man who has ever lived among the Copper Indians. It lies just as it was brought down last year (1885), in a soiled canvas bag, rudely marked with the words "U.S. Mail, Nuchuk."

John Bremner, the writer, joined the Allen Expedition in the spring of 1885, after wintering on the Copper River, and thence descended the Yukon River, as my friend Schwatka had done two years before. The intrepid prospector and plucky Yankee must be permitted to tell his own story "in his own quiet way," and in the language of his class, phonetically spelt and unpunctuated, but laconic, forcible, and unencumbered with redundant verbiage. The Copper Indians, as I was correctly informed by Professor Davidson of the Coast Survey, are considered the "most obstructive" of the coast tribes by the traders; and during their periodical visits to Nuchuk, which is their nearest trading store, twice or thrice a year, they are continually pilfering. Aleut watchmen are paid to guard the Company's property night and day during their stay. On the 29th of May 1885, the trader's diary contains the following entry—"Copper River Indians left to-day; they broke all the Government instruments, and raised h—— with everything about the place." They arrive in the spring and fall of the year in biderars, or wide, open skin boats, some of which they generally leave here for repairs. Sometimes their biderars are made with reindeer skins sewn over the framework, which they strip off and exchange for sealskins, which are more durable and are not procurable on the Copper River. On their last visit they sold to the Company nine hundred dollars' worth of furs, exchanging the money immediately after for goods, which they bought in bulk. Nicolai Rigoroff, the cook here, during a visit to their lower settlements on the river lately, baptized most of the tribe at the instigation of their medicine-man. He reported that they possessed a large hoard of furs in a cave at the cañon, and that no salmon were permitted to ascend the river beyond that point, which was barricaded with weirs. Instead of hunting much, they exchange salmon for furs with the tribes of the interior, for they have thus secured the monopoly of the fishing. Should a salmon succeed in passing the barrier, it becomes an object of frantic pursuit in the broad shallow stream, as they imagine it would be the means of stocking with young salmon the upper reaches of the river. But now let John Bremner tell his own tale.

Journal of a Trip up Copper River.

Sept. 1. Broke Camp about four o'clock and made six milles river good high mountins on the right bank and low glacier on the left.

Sept. 2. Started about six o'clock and made about twenty miles by the coursce of the river about twelvh miles in a strat line a low glacier on the West for about eaght miles when the river widend to five or six miles and verey shalow full of sand bares hordly passable.

Sept. 3. Started before sunrise and made about twenty-five miles by the course of the river wich bore more to the west verey shalow cut up in a great many channels and hordly passable a smawl came in on the East side and killed a large Mouse (*Moose*) and the Ma Nuska are stuffing it in to themselvs at a great rate.

Sept. 4. After georgeing themselvs with Mouse meat till about four o'clock the d—— rascals wanted to leave all my grub except one sack of flour and they would come back in the wenter and get it I told them no if they left my grub they hade to leave me to I did not prepose to trust my suplies out of my sight then they undertook to force me along but they found that uphill woark when they looked in the muszel of my revolver so they left me and said they would be back in ten days how I wish I had a few of the boys in blue here to teach them a lesson.

Sept. 5. Passed the day in the tent rained hard all day pleasent to be alone after a mounth in the Ma Nuska compney thare is a large opneing in the mountins on the west side of the river but so far of I cant tell if thar is a stream of aney sise comeing in about three 3 mils on the West side thar is a beautifull cascade apears to fall about one hundred feet.

Sept. 6. Remained in camp rained hard all day repaired some of my cloths and saw a pair of woodcock I dont know how thay make out to live here in winter.

Sept. 7. Went about ten miles to see that stream that I mencentioned comeing in on the East side it is about two hundred yards wide and not fordeable killed four ducks and am cooking one of them for my supper so you see I am liveing of the enemes contrey.

Sept. 8. I claimed the mountin back of camp

to get as good a viewe of the opening on the west side as I could it looks as if a large stream came in I expect it is the stream that heades in that lake that we were talking about though I could not get any information from the Ma Nuska thay claim to no notheng about it they talk about a river above Tarrayl that goes to salt water by makeing one-day's portage I dont go a cent on what thay say.

Sept. 9. Staid in camp all day a bear came prowling about camp last night could not get a shot at him it was so dark.

Sept. 10. Nothing to record onley that I am tormented with misquiters thar name is legion.

Sept. 11. A drove of Mouse passed close to camp in the night I shot at them by guess could not tell if I hit one or not this morning I went ant looked and saw whear one had bleed freely so I am going to track him up and see if I cant get him.

Sept. 12. I did not get my Mouse he had streangth enough to cross the river though he is dead enough by this I am sorry to lose so much meat but better luck next time.

Sept. 13. Alaska Bear are a fraud nothing but a hog except the pawes I tried yesterday all day to get in gunshot of an old one two cubes and failed thay are more timid then a rabbet.

Sept. 14. Rained hard all day so stayed in camp if the Ma Nuska dont come in two days more I shall go in to winter quarters build a cabin and weat till the river freases.

Sept. 15. Rained all day so stayed in camp.

Sept. 16. I expect I am stuck here for a while no sign of the Ma Nuska to-morrow I shall go to building a cabin.

Sept. 17. Rained all day stayed in camp and made me a cap.

Sept. 18. Rained hard all day I have given up looking for the Ma Nuska the d—— liers I will get even with them yet and dount you forget it.

Sept. 19. The Ma Nuska came last night so thay are better then I thought we will make another start for Tarrel to-day in the meantime they are stuffing themselves with beaver.

Sept. 20. Started about nine o'clock and made twelve miles the Ma Nuska killed there beaver on the way the valey narrowes in to about one mile in width snow caped mountins on each side the river is no account as a route for transportion shalow and rapid.

Sept. 21. Rained hard till about one o'clock when we started and did not camp till after dark made about ten miles the river verey rapid and shalow have to use the rope all the time a few scatring spruce but mostly cottonwood.

Sept. 22. Started about ten o'clock raining hard made about twelve miles the river verey rapid and shalow the valey betwen the mountins not more than half a mile wide scatring spruce and cottonwood on the hills near the river.

Sept. 23. Started about sunrise made about fifteen miles the river verey rapid hard work to get along the mountins not so high or ruged as they are further down the river.

Sept. 24. Got started about six o'clock and worked hard till after dark and made about ten miles the river verey bad the mountins geting lower as we get nearer the canyon the Ma Nuska say we will get to Tarral to-day I hope so for I am about wore out.

Sept. 25. We got an earley start and soon came to the canyon we had no trouble in going up through the river being so low the current wont so rapid as it was in a good maney placeses below I dont think the canyon is more then one mile long but when the river is high it must be a grand sight the river is comprest to about one hundred and fifty yards in weadth the sides being from fifty to one hundred feet high we are camped on the west side of the river whear theare is three houses we stoped hear to see the Tayon.

Sept. 25. He is a large stout-looking man but ston blind he was verey pertacler to find out what I wanted up hear but was satessfied that I wont going to take his throne away from him.

Sept. 26. Well I have got to the great city of Tarrall at last forty-seven days from Nu Chuck it is a h—— of river to navigate no good as a route to transport troops I went through the canyon again to-day and from whear the river first begines to narrow to the mouth is as near as I can estimate about two miles the city consistes of two houses and about forty-five or fifty inhabitants men women and children and thare is a good deal of spruce timber on the hills around here. The Chutânah comes in some distance above here I am going up to see it in a day or two.

Sept. 27. Nothing to record was buisey drying my stuff which had been wet for a long time I wont be able to get up the Chitana till it freases when Nicoli and four more men are going up and will help me get my grub up.

Sept. 28. Wourking hard fixing a place to winter in it froze water in the house.

Sept. 29. The Ma Nuska have all scaterd out up and down the river for the wenter they have no towne but houses hear and thar along the river.

Sept. 30. The river is full of floating ice this morning as cold as it is in November in God's contrey and the princeple food of the inhabitants is rabbets they apear to be a cross betwen the jack rabbit of the plains and comen cotentayl thar are lotes of them around here.

Oct. 1. Rained all day the weather haveing moderated havent seen the sun but once sence I have been hear.

Oct. 2. I am liveing alone not a native withen two miles I went out about sundown and killed five rabbits I am begining to live like the natives.

Oct. 3. The same dull rotine verey cold ice running in the river.

Oct. 4. Working on my house.

Oct. 5. Ditto.

Oct. 6. Ditto.

Oct. 7. Ditto.

Oct. 8. The river frozen over so that the natives cros it jamed in the canyon on the night of the sixth and raised the river ten feet.

Oct. 9. Snowed all day about six inches on a level.

Oct. 10. Very cold I expect it will be clear h—— before spring.

Oct. 11. Still very cold.

Oct. 12. Ditto.

Oct. 13. Moderated and pleasent.

Oct. 14. Snowing hard been at it all day and I have been with the negroes in Africa and the natives of Australa and among the Indians of the plains but of all the dirty divels I ever was with the Ma Nuska can beat them two to one. They take the hide of the rabbit and then boil him guts and all * * * * thar clothes are never taken of till they fall of or ruther rot of the wemen all take snuf and I have never seen one of them wash her hands or face since I have been hear so you can judge how thay look and still the men watch them like a cat would a mouse * * * *

Oct. 15. A pleasent day so I can go out without an overcoat. Three of the Ma Nuska dogs got in a air hole and went to the dog heaven or h—— more likely and they are making as much fuse about it as if it was three of theare young ones.

Oct. 16. Clear and cold nothing to record patching my old clothes.

Oct. 17. Bright cold day the Ma Nuska have just killed a bear on the other side of the river you would think h—— had broke loose if you heard the infearnel noise thay make.

Oct. 18. Clear but cold went out and killed rabbits all the afternoon.

Oct. 19. Snowed gentley all day fell about three inches.

Oct. 20. Had a veiset fron the Cheif's son a verey good-looking man for a Ma Nuska he lives about five milles up the river it is verey cold the natives all dress in fur I think I can stand the cold better than they can.

Oct. 21. Clear and cold.

Oct. 22. Thur is mourning in the camp No-til-nes passed in his checks this morning him and two others wear crossing the river at a place whear it is open and the raft capsized and he went under the ice I dont think thay make hordly so much fuss as thay did over the three dogs thay lost. It is not quite so cold to-day.

Oct. 23. Snowed gentley all day.

Oct. 24. Pleasent for this place. Two Col Chins came in from the headwaters of the Chitanah to-day one of them came to my hut and gave me a peace of native copper it is about one inch thick with rock atached to each side he says thar is mountins of it whear he got it I hope thar is I will find out how much thar is of it if I live.

Oct. 25. Clear but very cold my daley woark is to get wood to burn and kill rabbits to eat thar is no large game aurund here at preasent the natives say thar will be plenty of dear by un by thay say thar plenty of foxs but I have not seen a track so I dont think they are verey plenty.

Oct. 26. Clear but verey cold the floor of my cabin is frose two foot from the fire and I thought I had made it almost air tight so you see I am in no danger of melting with the heat. I saw the Volcano smoking for the first time to-day it is the mountin laid down on the chart as Mount Wrangle it dont look more than twenty-five or thirtey milles from here but the natives say it will take me three days to go thar I cant get one of them to go near it so I will have to go alone I sholl go as soon as the river is safe.

Oct. 27. Clear cold day went up to the mouth of the Chitanah it is about two miles above the head of the canyon it lookes to be about the same sise as the main river with a less rapid current the natives say it is a good stream to travel on no rocks or rapids on it I expect to go up in February when the ice is good I cant get a d—— one of the natives to show me the way to get to the Volcano thay say if I go thar I will die thay wont go within ten miles of it. As soon as the ice is safe I shall try and get thar by myself.

Oct. 28. Snowing hard nothing worth talking about the same thing over again every day.

Oct. 29. Snowed gentley all day the river has cut a chanel in the ice about one hundred feet wide and the current rushes through like a mill race the Ma Nuska say it will be another moon before it will be frozen so as to be safe to travel on.

Nov. 16. I have not writen aneything for some time it was the soame thing over and over every day. I made the atempt to get to the Volcano and failed I got within about one mile of the crater when one of my snow shoes broke and I came verey near passing in my checks before I could get back to the timber I froze several of my toes and my ears you ought to see them thay would match a goverment mules I dont think it is possible to make the ascent in the wenter but I think it would be easey in the summer I could not get ancy of the natives to go with me thay are all afraid to go ancy whear near it. I have been geting all the information about the natives I could but thay are verey shy about teling me aneything thay are scaterd along the river from the Canyon for about one hundred miles the houses from half a day to a day's travel apart and then the Col Chines are scaterd along the river above thar is fifteen houses scaterd along the river of the Ma Nuska as near as I am able to learn and opinion judging from the number of inhabtents in the houses I have been in I dont think thar is too exced one hundred of the Ma Nuska tribe men wemen and children thay get martin and foxes from the Col China and a verey little powder witch the Col China get on the Youcon and thar is onley one famley of Ma Nuska on the Chitanah the Col China are scaterd along the head waters and they go to Chitcat to trade and I wish you would inform the proper athortys that the traders at Chilcat are selling stricnyen to the Col China thay are no more fit to have poisen then a five year old child. The Ma Nuska are mostly armed with light double barrel guns or old Hudson Bay flent locks thay are very good marksmen considring the guns they have and in case of trouble with them thar powder would soon be spent and they could not get aney except at Newchuck or Chilcat and thay can't live away from the rivers one hundred white men could clean them out without much trouble animals would be no account light boats would be the onley thing that would do in the countrey it has not been so cold this month so far as it was in Oct. the river is still open eaghteen inches of snow on the level.

Nov. 28. This is a quire contry October was verey cold November has been quit pleasent a man could go around in his shirt sleaves and not feel cold it has rained all day to-day it has settled the snow so it is about a foot on a level before the rain thar has not been wind enough to shake the snow off the bushes since the first snow fell.

Oct. 29. Rained hard all day and is still at it I did not make my house rain proof and I am about drowend out.

Dec. 4. Pleasent I hant had a coat on for the last four weeaks and the Ma Nuska have been haveing a revulution after the fasion of thar white brothers the old Cheif had got poor and being old and blind he want able to fead the hungry divels that come to sponge on him and so thay toke his throne and gave it to another * * * it is looking bad for me the Ma Nuska have killed three Col China and the Ma Nuska are nearly scared out of wits thay just brought me a report that the Col China have murdered the store keeper that keeps the Co. store on the Uycon somewhear near the mouth of the Tinenah the Ma Nuska say it was Tinenah cuses that done it but they are such d—— liars I dont know wheather to beleave them ore not.

Dec. 5. Rained hard all day.

Dec. 6. Rain.

Dec. 7. Rain poured down all day water a foot deep in my house it hase raised the river seven fut the river dont look so much like freasing over as it did two months ago.

Dec. 8. Clear and freasing a little the Ma Nuska and the Col China are going to have a grand pow wow about one hundred miles up the river I want to go and see the player but the Ma Nuska say the Col China will kill me and then the Americans would come and kill them I shall go if I can.

Dec. 18. Clear and cold it remained pleasent till the fifteenth when it turned cold and is geting colder every day I have no means of teling how cold it is but I judge it has been from ten to fifteen below zero for the last three days. Things is looking bad the Col China have come to the Ma Nuska frontier and say thay are going to clean the Ma Nuska out a runner came in last night from the front he made the hundred milles in twenty-four hours the Tyon was at my cabin when he came and he came rushing in as if the divil was after him in less than an hour every man and boy old enough to handle a gun wear on the march up the river thay wouldnt let me go thay swor thay would tie me up if I tried to go the Tyon told me he did not think thar would be aney fighting he thought it would all end in talk but he promissed if thar was aney fighting to send for me so I am left the onley man in Taryel with all the wemen and children a fine dirty lot thay are.

Dec. 19. Cold.

Dec. 20. Cold.
Dec. 21. Ditto.
Dec. 22. Verey cold.
Dec. 23. Ditto.
Dec. 24. Not quite so cold.
Dec. 25. I wish you all a mercy Christmass I had rabbet for my diner insted of turkey the weather has moderated and it is quit pleasent no news from the seat of war.
Dec. 26. Pleasent.
Dec. 27. The river froze over.
Dec. 28. Pleasent.
Dec. 29. Pleasent.
Dec. 30. Pleasent.
Jan. 1, 1885. I wish you all a happey new year it is quit pleasent weather hear somewhear about zero but I do not fell it cold thar is not a breath of wind thar has been no stormey weather since the seventh of Dec. nor wind enough to stir a leaf and the war is over it all ended in talk and a big dance and I expect to start for the copper mines the midle of the month the natives say the ice will be good then I dont write much for the simple reason that thar is nothing to write about.
Jan. 2. Cloudy but not cold.
Jan. 3. Light fall of snow about one inch.
Jan. 4. Snowed hard all day fell eaght inches on the level but it is as light as down thar is not a breath of wind and the treas and bushes are loded with snow I have been haveing a little fun to breake

the monotoney of life at Tarrell the Ma Nuska have got it into thar heads that I am a big medicen and one of them came to my cabin earley yesterday to get me to go and see his wife he said she was going to die if I did not go and cure her I went with him about three miles through the snow and found that the most that alled the slut was dirt * * * I gave her eaght of Haynes piles and then made them strip her clothes of and scrub her from head to foot when they had got through scrubing her I made a mustard plaster * * * * * *
* her husband has been to my cabin to-day he says she is all right now he thinks me the boss medicen man I want the doctor when he writes to tell me if I treated the case properly.

Jan. 5. Clear and cold been patching my old clothes I expect I will be without clothes by the time I get back to Nuchuk.

Jan. 6. Verey cold this morning when I went to get up I found my whisker froze fast too my pelow and still I had slept warm and comfortable all night I wish I had some means of telling how cold it is and not a breath of wind.

Jan. 7. I had to roll out in the night to reef topsails the wind blowing a moderate gale from the north it is the first wind we have had in two months worth speaking of.

Jan. 8. Not quit so cold I had a vesit from a Col China to-day he told me thar was a hundred white men on the Youcon somewhear near the mouth of the Tanenah as near as I could make out he says they have gone into camp thar I expect that Sheglen found good digings thar and a porty have gone in to be ready in when spring opens I dont know what else would enduce white men to winter thar.

Jan. 9. Light brease from the north with light snow squalls not verey cold.

Jan. 10. Light snow squalls about zero I dont fell the cold aney more then I did at Newchuck the onley way I know it is so cold is if I toke my mitens of too fix a snare to catch a rabbit the ends of my fingers are froze in about five minuts.

Jan. 11. I had to go about four mils to-day to see a sick young one the fools think I can raise the dead.

* * * * * *

Thare was an old woman in the house in the last stage of consumption and the fools wanted me to cure her I told them that the Big Tyon up aloft said no that she must die and that I could not do aneything for her.

Jan. 12. Cold.

Jan. 13. Cold.

Jan. 14. Verey cold froze water three feet from the fire I went yesterday to see how the Ma Nuska preformed at a funral thay told me a young woman had died and thay weare going to burey her soon after I got thare one of the wemen began to chant a sort of tune in a low tone and preasently all hands joined in and thay kept geting louder and louder till I had to stuf my ears thay made such a noise after a while I thought I would have a look at the corpse I puled the cloth of her face and while I was looking she opned her eyes she want near as dead as thay had thought it apears she must have had some sort of a fit aneyway it bursted up the fun she lookes to be as likeley to live as aney of them when I left thay wear feeding her the soup from a rabbit's gutes.

Jan. 15. Verey cold.

Jan. 16. The cold is instense five feet above the fire the chemley is white weth frost.

Jan. 17. Cold cold cold.

Jan. 18. Still verey cold it would be all most imposable for troops to make a winter campaign the cold is so intense thay would all frease to death.

Jan. 19. Not quite so cold I have got the rheumatism in my right arm and shoulder, so I can hardley write.

Jan. 20. More moderate I can go out without freasing.

Jan. 21. Quite mild about zero I shall start in a few days for the copper contrey.

Jan. 22. Light snow squalls not verey cold.

Jan. 24. Quite mild light snow it has fell about three inches in the last forty-eaght hours.

Jan. 25. Pleasent not verey cold.

Jan. 26. Light squalls of wind from the north not cold.

THE VOLCANO IN ERUPTION.

Jan. 27. Warm wind from the south melting the snow it seames od too be able to go out in my shirt sleaves.

Jan. 28. Still thawing.

Jan. 29. Quit warm and pleasent the natives are cursing the warm weather it weats thar fur boots.

Jan. 30. Beautifull winter weather light wind from the south.

Jan. 31. Cloudy but warm and pleasent.

Feb. 1. Pleasent cloudy light wind from the north.

Feb. 2. The weather is still mild and pleasant the natives are scatring of from this place they squat here till they have eat all thar dried fish and stole nearley all my grub never hunted at all and now thay are half starved serves them right I wish thay weare more starved.

Feb. 3. A beautifull day not a cloud in the sky I was treated to a sight to-day that I wish you could have seen the volcano has been vercy quite (*quiet*) a good while but to-day it is sending out a vast colum of smoke and hurling imense stones hundreds of feet high in the air the mases it is throwing up must be vercy large to be seen here it is at least thirty milles in a air line from here to the mouth of the crater it has mde no loud reports onley a sort of rumbling noise.

Feb. 4. A little colder but pleasent the Volcano has stoped throwing stones ore makeing a noise but is still sending out an imense cloud of smoke it is verey beautifull not a breath of wind and the smoke ascends to a great hight in an imense colum before spreading out.

Feb. 5. Cloudy and colder light wind from the north the Ma Nuska have been promsing too start for Nuchuk for the two weeaks and thay hant started yet thay havent the least ideah of the value of time.

Feb. 6. Light snow about one inch thar was an old native came to my cabin to-day and I pumped him about that route too the lake he told me that two days' travel up the river thar was a river that headed in a large lake and one day's travel from the lake thar was a river that went to salt water but I think it must go into Cook's Inlet he says it goes to Nuchuk but from the lookes of the country I think its imposible the onley way to find out is to go and look the natives are such liars you cant trust aneything thay say.

Feb. 7. The natives have promised to start to-day I am lookeing for them every menuit so I will seal up the book.

P.S.—The natives are verey shy about telling a white man aneything about the country ore about themselves. What few Col China I have seen are a much finer looking people then the Ma Nuska I have been about fifty ore sixty miles up the river and as far as I can see it is as bad as it is below. The Canyon presents no obesticle to navegation at a modrate stage of water but below and above the river is uterley useless as a route to transport troops ore suplies in auey quanty and thar is another route from Chilcat that strikes the headwaters of the Chitanah but from all I can learn it is as bad as bad as Coper River the Col China pack through to Chilcat and it takes them two months to make the round trip. The natives all live along the rivers thay could not live aney great length of time back in the mountins. The countrey here is intierley difrent from the coast it is a dry climat verey cold in winter and verey hot in summer not a bad contrey to live in if it want for the rascals that live in it if the divil is the father of liars he has got a fine lot of children up here and as for stealing I defy the worald to produce a more expert lot of theives thay have stole nearley all my grub thay broke in to my cabin while I was away up the river and stole all my tea and sugar and two sacks of flour and worst of all nearly all my tobacco I have onley one sack of flour left no tea or sugar I have been liveing on rabbet strat for the last month. I wish if you can get it you would send me a small flag I would like too have the honur of raiseing the old Flag whar a white man has never been before at the Coper mine.

JOHN BREMNER.

CHAPTER XI.

Waiting at Nuchuk in Prince William Sound—The Indians refuse to move—We prepare to Winter there—The First Snow—Sport at Nuchuk—The Ducks, Grouse, and Geese—The Schooner arrives at last—Chenega and the Coast of the Kenai Peninsula—A Gale—We reach Kodiak—Fearful Murder at our Supper-table—A Terrible Passage to San Francisco—Homewards again.

> "And now the storm blast came, and he
> Was tyrannous and strong;
> He struck with his o'ertaking wings,
> And chased us South along."

NUCHUK, PRINCE WILLIAM SOUND, ALASKA,
September 22d, 1886.

THE last few weeks have been spent in short expeditions in the neighbourhood, partly for exploration and partly to keep us supplied with ducks and fresh salmon.

The schooner, our last chance of communicating with the outer world until the following spring, was expected to arrive here at Nuchuk, from the Alaska Company's eastern headquarters at Kodiak, between the 5th and 10th of September, with the winter supply of goods for the trading post.

Having now nearly given up all hope of its

arrival, I have made an attempt to procure men to take me by canoe to Kodiak in hopes of catching the steamer *St. Paul* on her way to San Francisco. It was therefore made known some days ago that two sealskin canoes and four men, or if that was

At Nuchuk; Gustia, once a Slave Boy.

not possible, one three-hatch canoe and men, were required to take me in the direction of Kodiak as far as was practicable, if only for a short way, and that any price they demanded would be paid. This evening the whole of the male inhabitants, together with the Tyoon, were summoned to the store, and the answer was then given by the Tyoon, through Nicolai, that at present no one was in want of money; also that there was no *astronome* to advise them concerning the weather; that soon Cook's Inlet would be frozen up, and that they did not wish to go by the outside passage.

The Alaskan Indians can never be counted on with certainty to work for money until driven by hunger to do so; and when they have just returned from a successful sea-otter hunt, as is now the case, they will only go where the caprice of the moment inclines them. Last year they omitted to dry sufficient salmon to last the winter, but this winter the trader has taken care that they have plenty.

Nuchuk, *September 29th.*

The Swedes, the two Carlsens, are preparing to return to their log cabin on Kaiak Island, in place of revisiting once more for the first time in ten years their home in Sweden, which they will now never be able to do, they say, and their winter will be passed as usual in sea-otter hunting.

I am preparing for a winter journey round Prince William Sound. I have bought a three-hole bidarky, and made some deerskin sleeping-bags,

PREPARING TO WINTER.

and succeeded in engaging one man. Most of the others are away on the islands trapping. With the prospect of five months winter I have had a long coat of squirrel skins made from two native *parkas* or sleeveless skin coats, which slip on over the head.

NUCHUK, *October 2d.*

Flocks of wild geese have been passing during the whole of the middle part of the day, without a break, flying southwards, band after band, in long rows.

NUCHUK, *October 9th.*

There has been snow on the mountains for some days. Last night the first snow fell at the settlement. I was camped out some miles away, and awoke in the morning to find everything hidden under a foot of snow outside the tent.

Sett-Shoo, a Boy of Oodiak. Dressed thus, he crossed the Pass, amid snow and ice, without requiring any other clothes.

We have been living on bear and wild-goat meat brought by the Indians from Tatockluk or Kancetluk villages in the sound, and on red salmon and ducks. I shot fourteen of the latter this morning, including mallard and blue-wing teal, with an old muzzle-loading trade gun, my own being still with the *Times* expedition.

We also shoot blue grouse occasionally in the woods; these birds are nearly always discovered perched on the fir-trees, and are difficult to find; also marmots near the mountain tops, from which there is a magnificent view of the sound. We also catch trout in a small pond near the village.

The wild geese would be easy to kill with a good gun, as they abound in the bay, and one can usually get a shot at thirty yards distance when one of the flocks alights on the hillside to feed.

Nuchuk, *October* 16*th*, 1886.

This morning we had just finished breakfast at daylight off our usual salt salmon and porridge, when I heard a shouting of "Sail, oh!"

These words had been shouted on so many previous occasions during the past eight weeks— sometimes at a tree floating with the tide, the bare projecting branches of which resembled masts; sometimes in jest, or at times at the fancied appearance of a sail on the horizon—that we took no notice. At last its loudness and persistence made us rush out. It was indeed the schooner. She was entering the bay in a thick fog—the first we have seen here. The two young Swedes for Kaiak are on board, and will just have time to get there by canoe before the Copper River freezes.

ON BOARD THE SCHOONER *Kodiak*, CHENEGA,
PRINCE WILLIAM SOUND, *October 20th*, 1886.

The schooner had been delayed during the

Knight's Island, from Five Miles North of Chenega, looking East.

summer partly by calms, and partly on account of an opposition company which has been started at Kodiak. Hence also our visit to Chenega, the western of the three Indian villages in Prince William Sound, in order to land a Creole trader to buy up all the sea-lion skins he can get, lest the competing party should obtain them.

The village itself lies under a steep wooded bluff.

We should never have found it had not a guide been brought from Nuchuk. This part of Prince William Sound consists of many steep mountainous islands—far more than are marked in the Russian chart, which is the only one in existence and which delineates groups of islands as one island. Their

Part of the Kenai Peninsula from Chenega.

southern sides are wooded and timbered, the northern sides being bare everywhere. Snow lies on the mountains down to the water's edge. In front of Chenega stretches a broad bay covered with small icebergs, and in which several whales are at this moment spouting. Close at hand several glaciers descend into the sea from the low flat snowfields visible on the high plateau of the mysterious Kenai Peninsula.

I recognise many of the Chenega Indians as having lately been over at Nuchuk trading.

Our guide will return in a skin canoe across the sound. We are just off for Kodiak, and thence for California, leaving winter behind us.

St. Paul, Kodiak Island, Alaska,
October 23d, 1886.

We have just reached this place after a severe passage. After getting clear of the islands we coasted along the south side of the Kenai Peninsula, obtaining glimpses through the clouds of several of the glaciers, which reach the ocean at five or six points of this rugged coast. Next day it blew a strong gale from the north-east—

> "Never did I like molestation view,
> Upon th' enchafed flood."

And although it was a fair wind for us, we had to lie hove to under close-reefed jib and close-reefed mainsail all that night, reaching this village, which is a comparatively civilised place, yesterday. It boasts a Russian church, and a well-to-do Creole and Indian population, living in substantial wooden houses, not huts, as elsewhere. It boasts also numerous large outhouses and stores of the Alaska Company, a schoolmaster, Customs (Ivan Petroff) and Signal Service Officers, with other white men. The Company's two steamers have left; we follow in the schooner on the 2d of November. All the vessels return here in April, and summer trade and hunting recommences then.

We were welcomed by Mr. B. G. M'Intyre, the general agent of this part (the eastern) of the Alaska Company's important business, not including the Fur Seal Islands. He accompanies us to San Francisco, and appears to be exceedingly popular with every one, for I have heard nothing of him except in praise. Meanwhile the schooner is to fetch a load of wood, and then we cross the Pacific.

At this time of year strong winds must be expected, but they are generally westerly—fair winds for us. The little schooner also is well-found, and with the Carlsons to help, will be well manned. The natives here still talk of the visit of Sir Thomas Hesketh's yacht, the *Paladine*, some years ago, and the ball that was given. I have to give a small one to-night.

St. Paul, Kodiak Island, Alaska,
November 3d, 1886.

The night before last I was the eye-witness to a shocking murder—none other than that of the general agent, whose corpse is on board. We start at noon for California, nearly two thousand miles distant.

We were seated at supper at six o'clock in the evening—M'Intyre at the head of the table, and Woche, a storekeeper, at the foot. Ivan Petroff was by my side. The meal was nearly over, and M'Intyre had half-turned to get up from his chair, when a terrible explosion suddenly occurred, filling the room with smoke and covering the table with fragments of plates and glasses.

M'Intyre never moved, for he was killed stone-dead in a moment. Woche fell under the table, and then rushed out streaming with blood in torrents, for he was shot through the lower part of the head. The double glass window was smashed to atoms, for a cowardly fellow had fired through it, from just outside, with a spreading charge of slugs, presumably aiming at M'Intyre, who received the main part of it in his back. Meantime the murderer who had thus shot into a group of unarmed and unsuspecting persons had time to escape.

I succeeded in stopping the bleeding from Woche's wounds, every one appearing paralysed!

The suspected man, Peter Anderson, a Cossack of the Don, cannot be found. He had, we found, attempted to fire his sloop, lying at anchor near the wharf; and had refused employment at cod-fishing, in order, as he said, to be present at the departure of the schooner. He had also been seen loitering with a gun behind the house. He owed money to M'Intyre, who had twice fitted him out for sea-otter hunting, but both times he was unsuccessful.

We have been scouring the woods with rifles, but the natives are frightened to death. Not a light can be seen in any house after dark for fear of its being shot into by this madman, who is still at large if he has not committed suicide. Nor can any of them be got to stir out at night, or to keep watch like sentries over the sloop, in case he should return, unless a white man is with them.

On Board the Schooner *Kodiak*,
San Francisco Harbour, *November 16th*, 1886.

We arrived last night after the most uncomfortable twelve days I ever endured. For two nights we lay hove to in fearful gales, while during the latter part of the voyage a terrible stench in the cabin, probably from bilge water and the salt salmon in the hold, forced me to live in the forecastle with the three sailors, who were exceedingly attentive. This made up to some extent for the behaviour of the captain, who was mad drunk, and abusive of England, and insulting to every one. He took it into his head at last that I had gone to the forecastle to obtain from the sailors grounds of complaint against him.

I cannot close this journal without acknowledging the politeness of the Alaska Commercial Company, and the hospitality received through their employés at Nuchuk and Kodiak.

SAN FRANCISCO, *November 30th*, 1886.

The little 70-ton schooner *W. Sparkes* has just arrived from Alaska, having left Kodiak on the 9th. The murderer has not been found. I leave to-morrow for England.

APPENDIX.

The Fur Trade of Alaska—Fur-seals—Hair-seals—Sea-Lions—Sea-otters — Prospects of the Fur Trade a Century ago as estimated by Cook—The Varieties of Foxes—Black and Brown Bears—Their Pursuit—The Lynx, Polar Bear, Marten, Cariboo, Moose, Sheep, and Goat—Prince William Sound and its Indians—A Description of Cook's Inlet and its Shores—The Fur-trading Stores—The Volcanoes—Cape Douglas—A Description of the Alaskan Peninsula, its Settlements, Game, and Mountains—Unexplored Alaska—Future Sporting Expeditions—A Chugamute Vocabulary.

THE ALASKAN FUR TRADE.

From 1870 to 1880 the furs bought by traders from natives were as follows:—

	$	c.	
40,283 sea-otter @	60	0	each
19,000 land-otter @	2	50	,,
41,217 beaver @ .	2	50	,,
6992 black fox @ .	15	0	,,
19,210 cross fox @	2	50	,,
82,919 red fox @ .	1	0	,,
7508 blue fox @ .	2	0	,,
11,491 white fox @	1	0	,,
819 black bear @ .	3	0	,,
5207 brown bear @	1	50	,,
71,213 mink @ .	0	20	,,
81,609 marten @ .	2	0	,,
50,322 musk rat @	0	5	,,
6312 lynx @ .	2	0	,,
421 wolf @ . .	1	50	,,

The Alaska Commercial Company have the sole right of killing fur-seal, which are almost entirely confined to the two small islands of Prybilof, lying north of the Aleutian chain of islands. The chief season is in May. The natives may also kill fur-seals. The hair-seal and sea-lion skins are chiefly used in making the skin canoes. The sea-otters, however, are still the chief objects of pursuit. Their skins have varied in value from ten dollars in the time of the Russians up to two hundred dollars. Their pursuit by the Indians with bows and arrows in the skin canoes, and the exhaustion of the animal by not allowing it time to breathe, and its death, have been fully described by Mr. Elliott in his account of the Sea Islands, and by Ivan Petroff, who was seated next me during the fearful murder at our supper-table of the general agent of the Alaska Commercial Company, in his report upon Alaska (U.S. 10th Census, 1880).

The value of a good sea-otter skin is now something under a hundred dollars. They are becoming scarcer. A century ago Cook wrote with regard to the natives:— "I will be bold to say the Russians have never been amongst them, for if that had been the case we should hardly have found them clothed in such valuable skins as those of sea-otters. There is not the least doubt that a very beneficial fur-trade might be carried on with the inhabitants of this vast coast. But unless a northern passage could be found practicable it seems rather too remote for Great Britain to receive any emolument from it." He adds that "intercourse with foreigners would increase their wants by introducing them to an acquaintance with new luxuries, and in order to be able to procure these they would be more assiduous in procuring skins." How fully this has been verified!

Black or silver and cross foxes are not confined to any particular district, and are trapped everywhere in small numbers, but chiefly in the country of the Chilcats, and the upper part of the Copper River, and the Kenai Peninsula. A trader will pay as much as fifty dollars for a good skin.

The white and the blue Arctic foxes are more plentiful in the north. The red fox is common everywhere.

The brown bear of Alaska (*ursus Richardsonii*) seems to prefer an open swampy country to the timber. His northern limit is about 67° N. Ivan Petroff describes the brown bear as "the great road-maker of Alaska." His tracks line the banks of the stream. Their skins are commercially of no value except when killed in winter. During summer they frequent the salmon rivers in immense numbers. They are rarely hunted. John Ingster of Winnipeg, who spent two years on Sanak Island hunting sea-otters, and others, have informed me that they have seen over twenty together near the mouths of rivers during the run of the salmon. The Indians assert that bears swarm at Lake Nushegak, while Petroff includes the country between that lake and the lower Kuskoquim River. They are undoubtedly very numerous on the island of Unimak or Oonimak, and on the Alaskan Peninsula. Kodiak Island is full of them. Cook's Inlet abounds with bear of the largest size, where, says Petroff, " on the steep sides of the volcanic range on the west coast brown bear can be seen in herds of twenty or thirty; their skins are not valuable, and owing to this fact, and to the fierce disposition of the animals, they are not commonly hunted." The black bear is confined to the timber on the mainland and on a few of the large islands in Prince William Sound. Near the vol-

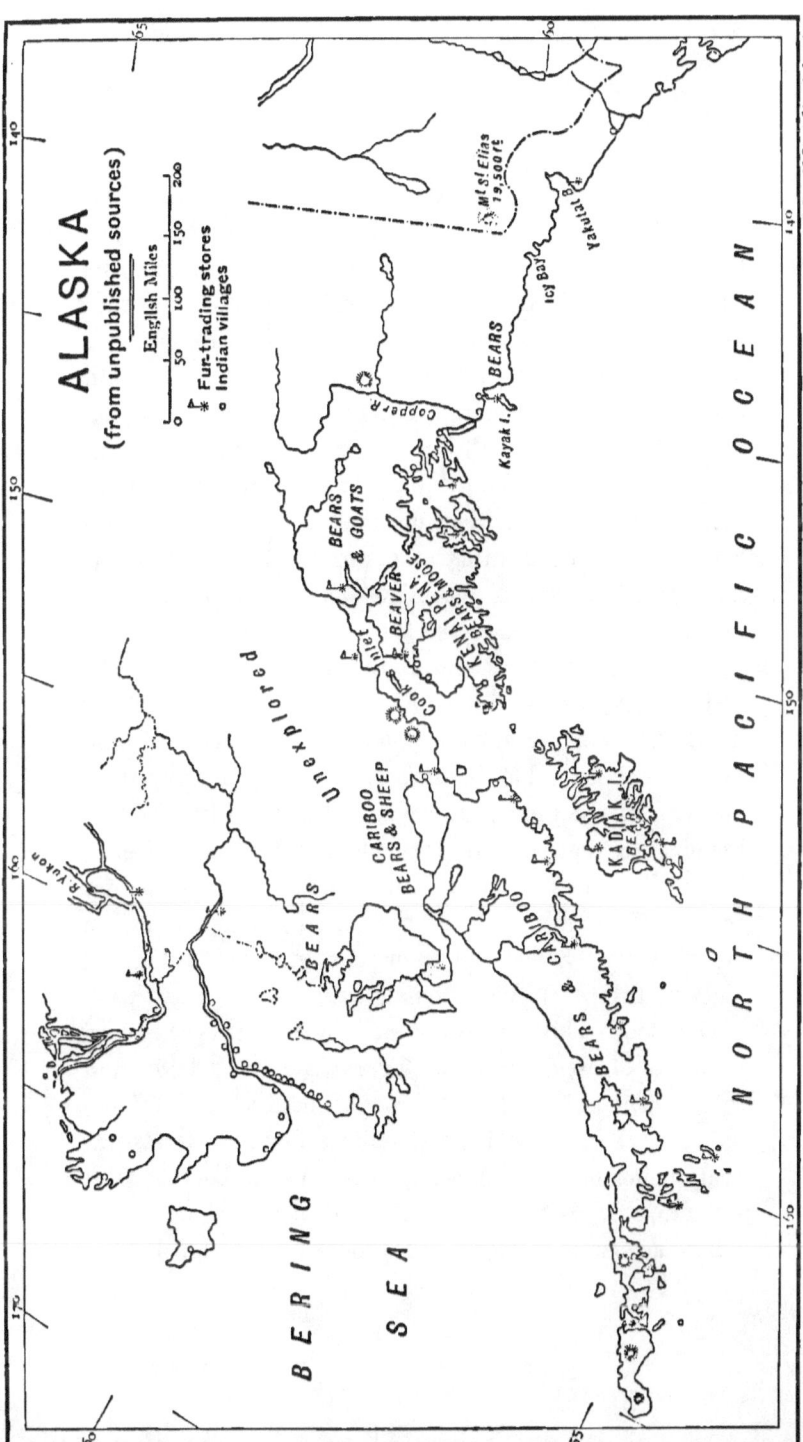

canoes game is particularly abundant, for no Alaskan Indian will approach a volcano, and the wild animals instinctively congregate there.

From one end of the Alaskan Peninsula to the other lie well-beaten tracks of the reindeer. Bears follow in their trails whenever they congregate in large numbers. The bears have a habit when wounded of attacking their assailant, which is unfortunate for the bad shot. A Winchester repeating rifle is commonly used. "See him come!" calmly ejaculated one of the traders who had fallen in (or out) with bruin near Katmai, and whose magazine was still half full; "he's so ballasted up on both sides with lead that he can't fall over." A rifle, however, of more destructive power and of larger calibre than a Winchester is desirable—one throwing a bullet that will reach and paralyse the great nerve-centres when the enemy is hit anywhere in the fore-part of the body.

The lynx is found in the Kenai Peninsula and St. Elias Alps. The Polar bear is only found on the Arctic Coast. The marten or sable (*mustela Americana*) is trapped on the Alps of the Copper River and Prince William Sound. Reindeer or cariboo are very plentiful on the Alaskan Peninsula and in Cook's Inlet, as well as in the far north. Moose are found on the Kenai Peninsula, and in the interior. Sheep are numerous in Cook's Inlet, and goats in Prince William Sound.

Our food while we were at Nuchuk in the sound consisted of wild ducks and geese, and of salmon and wild goat, and bear meat brought occasionally by the Indians. But while Prince William Sound is comparatively deficient in large game, Cook's Inlet abounds with it. From St. Elias to Chugach or Prince William Sound (where are three villages), the people only number 600.

Seal meat and mountain goat are eaten in equal proportion with salmon. The Chugamutes are Christians, and have built a small Russian church at Nuchuk, to which they contribute a proportion of sea-otter skins.

At the head of Prince William Sound is a portage of a day's travel to Cook's Inlet, which was crossed by Petroff, and where he saw moose in May. Two glaciers are crossed on the way.

In Prince William Sound Vancouver's parties (1794) found some Indians "who had come immediately from Groofgincloof or Cook's Inlet, and that *they with their canoes had crossed the isthmus overland that separates this sound from Turnagain Arm.*"

Cook's Inlet (discovered by Captain Cook), which has been called Summerland by the traders, from the constant fine weather during the summer, is inhabited by 800 natives and a few half-breeds, relics of the old Russian American Company, who fish exclusively from May to September. The east side is formed by the Kenai Peninsula.

In 1850 the Keknu River was ascended by Lt. Doroshin, and in 1879 by Ivan Petroff up to the Skilloch village of Kenaitze Indians, who kill a few beaver in the lakes. He informed me they were great travellers, and that the women carried packs. At the mouth of the Keknu River is a school and a salmon cannery of the Cutting Packing Company, and the fur post of Fort Kenai. Some miles south is the Kassiloff River salmon fishery. Near the end of the Peninsula of Kenai are the two fur posts and stores of Saldovy and English Bay. The west shore of the peninsula is flat and low, but the east coast is rocky and indented with bays, in one of which (Resurrection Bay) an American hunter has built a log-house, and resides.

The mountains rise to a height of 6000 feet, and are covered with low flat glaciers and snow-fields. Turnagain Arm, where the portage from Prince William Sound ends, is bordered by high mountains, reaching 7000 feet on the north side near the estuary of the Knik River, where are situated some Tinnat Indian villages. The winter post of the Alaska Commercial Company is in the Knik Inlet, where in 1885 the storekeeper Holt was shot by an Indian. The numbers of mosquitoes in summer cause the store to be removed at that season to an island in the estuary of the river.

Vancouver says, in regard to some Indians of Cook's Inlet:—" I should be wanting in justice to our Indian passengers, were I to omit stating their docility and respectful behaviour, and the real satisfaction and happiness they exhibited on being given to understand that we were again in perfect security."

On the west shore of Cook's Inlet is the A. C. C. post of Tyonik. The mountains are wooded up to 1000 feet. To the south lie Burnt Mountain Volcano, and next to it Iliamna Volcano (12,060 feet), on the shore of which Mr. Petroff once landed, but found the ascent too steep to attempt, even as far as the crater, which is below the summit.

Vancouver noted Mount Ilyamna:—" In the middle appeared the volcano, near the summit of which, from two distinct craters on its south-eastern side, were emitted large volumes of whitish smoke, unless, as was supposed by some, it was vapour arising from hot springs in that neighbourhood." He calls St. Augustin "a very remarkable island."

Some miles south a portage leads from the sea to the large Ilyamna Lake, where there is a store kept by a half-breed. Opposite lies Augustin Island in active eruption. At the entrance to Cook's Inlet the tides run with great violence.

Cook discovered Cook's Inlet, and it obtained his name. He named the boldest cape in Alaska Cape Douglas, after the then Canon of Windsor—" a very lofty promontory, whose elevated summit, forming two exceedingly high mountains, was seen above the clouds."

From this point to the extremity of the Alaskan Peninsula the shores are rocky and sparsely inhabited. At intervals of about sixty miles are situated the A. C. C. posts of Douglas, Katmai, Wrangel, Sitkoom, Matrofan, Belkoffsky, and Majovy. The great cod-banks on the coast are unworked. From Cape Douglas westward timber is confined to the interior, and near Wrangel all timber ceases. Belkoffsky is a large village of sea-otter hunters, chiefly Scandinavians. The volcano of Pavloff was in very active eruption in August 1886. Majovy is at the extreme end of the peninsula, near which the Indian or Aleut village of Morshevoi holds a hundred dissolute inhabitants, who, according to Petroff, have not even the energy or cleanliness to make use of some hot springs half a mile distant. The groups of islands opposite Belkoffsky are the resort of sea-otters, and contain settlements of white hunters at Unga, Gusina, Siminosky (in the Shumagin group), and Popoff, where M'Collam & Co. have a cod-fishery. Unimak is the first of the Aleutian Islands. It is bare and rocky, and the volcanoes on it are active—Mount Shishaldin (9000 feet) and Mount Progomny (5000 feet). Since the Russian massacre a hundred years ago, the natives have held superstitions with regard to it, and it has been totally uninhabited. It is said to swarm with the common red fox and a species of wolf. Bear are very numerous on it, and it is the only Aleutian island frequented by reindeer or cariboo, which are able to pass the narrow straits which divide it from the mainland.

Akutan is the next Aleutian island; then comes Unalaska, with a large settlement of whites. Two hundred miles to the north lie the two fur-seal islands, St. George and St. Paul, while the wind-swept chain of the Aleutians stretches out to Asia. The north side of the Peninsula of Alaska is well-nigh uninhabited, and is the resort of walrus. The mountains rise in groups from five to eight thousand feet. The glaciers are all high up, and the numerous portages lead across flat swampy plains between Bering Sea and the North Pacific. Kodiak, the largest island, is separated from the peninsula by Shelikoff Straits, and boasts the white settlement of St. Paul, besides several half-breed and Indian villages, and the salmon-fishery of Karluk.

The Alaskan Peninsula and Cook's Inlet are undoubtedly great game countries. The fleet of trading schooners and sealing steamers for Unalaska and Kodiak leave San Francisco early in March. The country to the west of Cook's Inlet is entirely unexplored, but Indian report represents it as a land of lakes and of high mountains.

An expedition probably unequalled for its novel scenery and for sport with bear, cariboo, and ptarmigan, would consist in coasting in a bidarky from Katmai to Unga, where there is constant communication by trading schooners, while a field quite as attractive is offered by the west coast of Cook's Inlet and by the volcanic region near it. The only drawback is the impracticable nature of the natives, half-breed and Indian, and the necessity of the party being constituted in such a way as to be independent of their aid.* The natives of the head of Cook's Inlet, however, unlike the inhabitants of the Alaskan shore-line, are of the Athabascan or Inland tribes of North American Indians, and expert as hunters, travellers and mountaineers, inhabiting also part of the Kenai Peninsula and trading with the interior. It is to be hoped that soon regular communication will be established between Sitka and Kodiak, two days' steaming, while at present the voyage from San Francisco to the latter place takes nearly a fortnight.

* See the *Fortnightly Review* for March 1887, "A Fresh Field for the Sportsman."

A VOCABULARY

OF USEFUL WORDS IN THE LANGUAGE OF THE CHUGAMUTES OR NATIVES OF PRINCE WILLIAM SOUND.

Syllables in *italics* pronounced gutturally.

One, atoojuk.
Two, ah-tlak.
Three, ping-i-cuk.
Four, setar-mik.
Five, tar-tlee-mik.
Six, ah-cooin-dlin.
Seven, mar-tl-hōmin.
Eight, ee-gloo-glin.
One dollar, tlar-heema-nageet.
Twenty-five cents, ageet-stur-tuk.
Fifty cents, dingai-uk-coop-loogoo.
Much money, amlik-toot-ageet.
How much, cow-ouchin.
Too much, am*lach*-pig*ach*-toot.
Too little, eekow-pag*ach*-toot.
A little money, cek-owdoot-ageet.
Out, tlar-me.
In, eeloom-e.
To-day, ag*och*-n*ach*-p*uck*.
To-morrow, oo-norgo.
Day after to-morrow, ya-teego.
After, } takoo.
Later, }
Go back, oot*ach*-ten.
What is the name? narma-ut-krur.
Never mind, tchan-ee-dok.
Come, ti-ee-hoot.
Go, agwar.
Eat, pee-doo-ah.
Drink, umm-ah.
Sleep, shah-gah.
Give me, too-neeg-nah.
Flowing tide, eel-ah-loo-go.
Ebbing tide, eel-eeg-loo-go.
Good, ash-ek-dok.
Bad, ash-ee-dok.
Long, tak-oke.

Short, neneedok.
Hungry, kieech-ktwar.
Slow, ishow-la-marsuk.
Quick, tschoo-gar.
Thirsty, muk-*sooch*-ktwa.
Bear, loklok.
Wild goat, soo-park.
Mink, eel-gwark.
Sea-otter, eegum-ark.
Hair-seal, kai-ark.
Fur-seal, ah-tuk.
Sea-lion, wee-na.
Fox, ko-gwee-ak.
Deer, hunnai-ak.
Duck, oomooshuk.
Goose, tem-oo-yak.
Grouse, ung-ai-ik.
Fish, am*ach*-too.
Man, schook.
Woman, ah-gun-uk.
Boy, tar-new-hungwar-shuk.
Girl, karnee-klungwar-shuk.
Tree, nego-gwar-tak.
Spear, ho-kk.
Boat, yalik.
River, gweek.
Sea, ee-*march*-peck.
Matches, speetch-kee.
Bread, kleba.
Flour, mooka.
Meat, kmook.
Sugar, sarka.
Tea, tchai.
Tent, palatkuk.
Bed, ash-lo-uk.
Fire, kuuk.

INDEX.

ADAMS, U.S.S., 54, 55, 56
Akutan, 242
Alagnuk, 171
Alaska Commercial Company, 52, 54, 127, 131, 140, 194, 197, 198, 222, 230, 232, 235
Alaskan Peninsula, 242
Albert Cañon, 14
Alps of Alaska, 48-50
Andersens, the, 52, 144, 150, 152
Anderson, Peter, the murderer, 232
Ascending Mount St. Elias, 101-104
BALLOW, Dr., 52
Barometrical measurements, 84, 103, 104, 112, 113
Beardslee Island, 38
Bear Hunter, 67, 127, 129
Bears, 34, 104, 114, 149, 150, 151, 164, 165, 179, 196, 204, 225, 234, 236, 237, 238, 242
Bears in British Columbia, 24
Bears in the Canadian National Park, 8
Bear tracks, 68, 71, 72, 76, 77, 80, 96
Beaver, 205
Beaver Cañon, 12
Beechey, 75
Berries, 52, 71, 74, 125, 197
Behms Canal, 30
Belcher, 105
Belkoffsky, 148, 153, 241
Bering, 105
Bidarkies, 185, 186, 187
Big Bend, 11
Blacktail, 42
Blacktail deer on Vancouver Island, 24
Boots worn out, 99
Boundary-line, 64
Bremner, John, 200-221
British Columbia, growth of, 25
Buffalo bones, 3
Bursting of a river, 95, 113, 114

CALGARY, 3
Campaigner with General Gordon, 17
Canadian Pacific Railway, 1
Cañons of the Thompson and the Fraser, 19
Cape Douglas, 241
Cape Phipps, 123
Cape St. Elias, 142, 143
Cape Suckling, 140, 141, 150
Cape Whitshed, 169, 170, 172
Cariboo, 238, 242
Cariboo Mines, 17
Carlsen, Louis, 52, 224, 230
Carlsen, Olaf, 53, 145, 224, 230
Carlsens, the, 224, 230
Cascade Mountain, 9
Castani, Lake, 89
Castle Mountain, 9
Cat-fish, 41, 42
Cathedral Mountain, 9, 10
Cattle country of British Columbia, 17
Cattle country of Canada, 3
Chenega, 227, 228, 229
Chichagoff I., 47
Chief of the Copper Indians, 206, 214
Chief of the Yakatats, 54, 55, 56, 124, 125
Chilcat and Chilcoot, 36, 161
Chinamen, 16
Chinese in British Columbia, 23
Chitanah River, 210, 212
Coast Survey, 48-50, 75, 106, 111
Cod-banks unworked, 241
Col Chins, 210, 212-214
Columbia River, 11
Controller's Bay, 162
Copper River Indians, 83, 163, 167-171, 200-221
Copper River, 227
Cook, 105, 143, 162, 194, 198, 199, 235, 239, 241
Cook's Inlet, 224
Cross Sound, 47

INDEX.

Dalton, 46, 69, 114, 119, 129, 130
Davidson Glacier, 36
Davidson, Prof., 200
Death of M'Intyre, 231, 232
Deaths of Indians, 130, 133, 209, 210
Departure from Victoria, 19
Devil's Head, 5
Devil's Lake, 6, 7
Dixon Entrance, 26, 29
Dog-fish, 41, 42, 146
Dogs, Indian, 128, 148
Donald, 12
Doroshin, Lt., 239
Douglas, 241
Ducks, 226
Duke of Clarence Straits, 30
Dumbough, Lieut., 66
Eagle Glacier, 36
Eagle Pass, 2, 15, 16
Elk on Vancouver Island, 24
Elliot, 235
English Bay, 239
Esquimault, 23
Fairweather Ground, 66
Farwell, 14
Fee Springs, 78
Fishing at Sitka, 40, 41, 42
Fishing in the Bow, 4
Fishing in The Devil's Lake, 7
Fording rivers, 73, 74, 84
Forest fires, 16, 42
Fort Macleod, 3
Fort Simpson, 29
Fort Tongass, 29
Fort Wrangel, 30
Foxes, 234, 236, 237, 242
Fraser River, 18, 19
Furs, 201, 234, 235-239
Fur-trade of Alaska, 234, 235-239
Gales, 229, 232, 233
Game on Vancouver Island, 24
Geese, 195, 196, 225, 226
Glacial measurements, 38
Glaciers, extent of, 63, 64, 110, 111, 38
Glaciers of the Copper River, 169-171
Goat Peak, 9
Goats, 89, 196, 225
Gold in British Columbia, 12
Gold-mining, 34, 35, 55
Gold Range, 15, 16
Golden City, 11
Great Agassiz Glacier, 56, 84, 122, 123

Great Guyot Glacier, 75, 78, 80, 111, 138
Great Tyndall Glacier, 98, 101, 102, 110
Griffin Lake, 17
Grouse, 226
Gusina, 241
Halibut hook, 196
Harrisburg, 34, 35, 46
Hats, 60, 61
Hawkins Island, 172-177
Heights, table of, 112, 113
Hesketh, Sir T., 230
Highest timber bridge in the world, 12
Hinchinbrook Island, 177, 179-227
Holt, murder of George, 131, 240
Hot springs, 8, 9
Howkan, 30
Humming-bird, 81
Hyamna Lake, 241
Hydahs, 23
Ice axes, 70
Icy Bay, 56, 64, 65, 72, 134, 137
Icy Cape, 79, 137, 138, 139
Idaho, s.s., 44
Illecillewaet River, 13, 14
Indian carvings, 21
Indians, drunken, 53, 166
Indian houses, 156, 157
Indian wares, 40
Indian races, 194, 195, 243
Indians of Queen Charlotte Islands, 23
Indians of Vancouver Island, 23
Indians, threatening, 53
Ingster, John, 236
Inland passage, 26
Islands of Prince William Sound, 228
Italian Geographical Society, 89
John Bremner, 200-221
Jones River, 75, 79, 81, 82
July 4th at Sitka, 43, 63
Juneau City, 34, 35, 46
Kaiak Island, 52, 54, 127, 140, 142-162
Kam'cyga, 186
Kamloops Lake, 18
Kassiloff River, 239
Katmai, 238, 241-243
Keknu River, 239
Kenai, 179, 228, 229, 239, 243
Kursunk, 46, 92
Kicking Horse Pass, 10, 11
Klok-Shegees, 159
Knight's Island, 227

INDEX. 247

Knik River, 131, 240
Kodiak, 54, 155, 229-232, 242
Kodiak, schooner, 227-230, 232, 233
Kruzoff I., 42
Kuskoquim River, 236
LAKES, Glacier, 89, 97, 98
La Perouse, 105, 140
Leases of cattle lands, 4
Length of transit by Canadian Pacific Railway, 2
Libbey, Prof. W., 20, 46, 63, 69, 70, 81, 90, 92, 93, 96, 97, 114, 126, 129, 130
Loops of the Canadian Pacific Railway, 14
Loring, 30
Lynn's Canal, 36
Lynx, 234, 238
Lytton, 18
MALASPINA PLATEAU, 56, 111
Ma-Nuska, 202, 221
Masks, 57, 60
Matrofan, 241
Majovy, 241
M'Intyre, B. G., 230, 231, 232
Medicine hat, 3
Medicine man, 59, 128, 160, 129-133, 165, 169
Metlakatla, 29
Middleton Island, 187
Moose, 202, 204, 238, 239
Moose-jaw, 3
Moraines, 77, 78, 81, 84, 85, 111
Morshevoi, 241
Mountain goats, 29, 33
Montague Island, 193
Mount Begbie, 14
Mount Carrol, 12
Mount Cook, 50, 51, 99
Mountain Creek, 12
Mount Crillon, 38
Mount Edgcumbe, 39, 42
Mount Fairweather, 38, 47, 48, 50
Mount Hector, 9
Mount Hermit, 12
Mount Ilyamna, 240
Mount La Perouse, 38
Mount Lefroy, 9
Mount Malaspina, 51
Mount Progomny, 241
Mount Shishaldin, 241
Mount Sir Donald, 13
Mount Stephen, 9
Mount St. Augustin, 240, 241
Mount St. Elias, ii. v., 49, 50, 56, 63, 102, 105-109, 122

Mount Vancouver, 50, 51
Mount Wrangel, 106, 210-212, 219
Mountain Goats, 24
Muir's Glacier, 37, 38
Murder of M'Intyre, 231, 232
Murders, 55, 131, 231, 232, 240
NANAIMO, 29
Nanaimo Mines, 20
Nasty customs, 149, 157, 159, 208
Native dances, 182-185
New York Times Expedition, 20, 37, 43, 44
Nicholls, Commander, 46, 63, 66
Norwegians, 151
Nuchuk, 179-227
OCEAN CAPE, 48, 123
Oodiak, 170, 171, 195, 225
PACIFIC COAST NAVIGATION COMPANY, 26
Paludine, yacht, 230
Parka, 225
Pavloff, 241
Peril Straits, 39
Petroff, Ivan, 150, 195, 230, 231, 235, 236, 239
Pinta, U.S.S., 36, 46, 48, 51, 56, 62-127
Point Martin, 162-166, 169
Polar Bear, 238
Port Etches, 180
Port Hammond, 19
Prairies of Canada, 3
Pribiloff Island, 242
Prince William Sound, 54, 179, 187, 193, 227, 228
Ptarmigan, 188
Punishing Indians, 46
QUEEN CHARLOTTE SOUND, 26
Quicksands, 76, 83, 114
RABBITS, 212
Reindeer or Cariboo, 17
Resources of British Columbia, 25
Revelstoke, 14
Revilla Gigedo Island, 30
Rogers Pass over the Selkirks, 2, 11-13
Royal Geographical Society, 69, 139
Russian Company, 39
Russian Bath, 192, 193
Russian church at Nuchuk, 180, 184, 185
SABLE, 234, 238
Saldovy, 239
Salmon, 167, 175, 176, 177, 188-192, 195, 196, 202, 239
Salmon-fishing, 41, 189

INDEX.

Salmon on Vancouver Island, 24
Sanak, 236
Scenery, Alaskan, 178, 179
Scenery at Yakatat, 48
Schwatka, Lieut., 20, 45, 70, 73, 75, 79, 93, 101, 103, 104, 130, 200
Scientific instruments, 69, 99, 100, 116, 126
Sea-birds, 52
Sea-lions, 195
Seals, 68, 71, 72, 135, 155, 195, 234, 235
Sealskins, 155, 201, 234, 235
Sea-otters, 135, 136, 152-155, 158, 185, 197, 198, 234, 235, 241
Second crossing of the Columbia, 15
Selkirk Range, 12-14
Seton Karr, H. W., 46, 79, 81, 90, 101, 103, 231, 232
Sett-Shoo, 225
Shuswap Indians, 17
Shuswap Lakes, 17
Sikamous Narrows, 17
Sitkoom, 241
Sitka, 39, 43, 44, 46, 47, 63
Shawaan, 59, 160, 128, 129-133, 162, 165, 169
Sheep, 238
Skeena River, 29
Skilloch Lake, 239
Spellumacheen River, 17
Sporting expeditions, 242, 243
Squirrel-skins, 225
St. George Island, 242
St. Elias Alps, 141
Stephen's Passage, 33
Stikeen River, 30
St. Paul Island, 242
Stony Creek, 12
Stony Indians, 6
Strawberries, 52, 71, 74, 125, 197
Surf, 65, 66, 115-123, 160
Surf, launching in the, 115-122
Swans, 68
Swedish traders, 52, 127, 140, 144
Syndicate Peak, 13

Taku Inlet, 33, 44
Tateekluk, 225
Tebenkoff, 75, 105
The s.s. *Ancon*, 19
Thompson Rivers, N. and S., 18
Three Brothers, schooner, 127, 134-144
Timber, 35, 36, 228
Timber of Prince William Sound, 228
Timpseans, 23
Totem poles, 20, 26, 30
Trading material, 54
Trading with Indians, 59, 125, 140, 197, 198, 201
Trout-fishing at Griffin Lake, 17
Trout-fishing in Kamloops Lake, 18
Trout-fishing on Vancouver Island, 24
Tyonik, 240
Unalaska, 54
Unexplored Alaska, 242
Unga, 241, 243
Uninnak Island, 236
Valley of the Bow, 5
Vancouver, 19, 20, 75, 105, 179, 239, 240
Vancouver Island, 20, 23, 24
Victoria, 19, 20, 23, 24
Vocabulary of Chugamute, 244
Volcanoes, 210, 211, 212, 219, 236, 237, 238, 240, 241
Western notices, 14
Whales, 228
Wind, 155, 156, 173
Winnipeg, 2
Woche, 231, 232
Woodcock, 203
Woods, 46, 69, 79, 81, 94, 95, 101, 103, 104, 115, 119
Wrangel, 241
Wrangel Straits, 30
W. Sparkes, schooner, 233
Yagtag, Cape, 67
Yakatat, 48-56, 67, 71, 124
Yale, 19

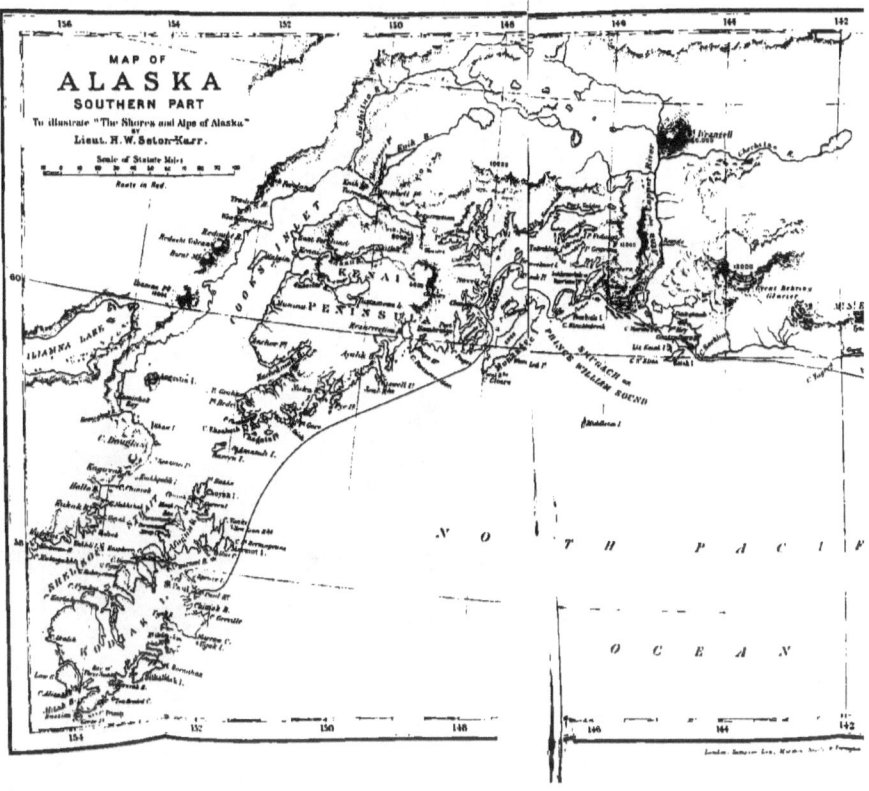

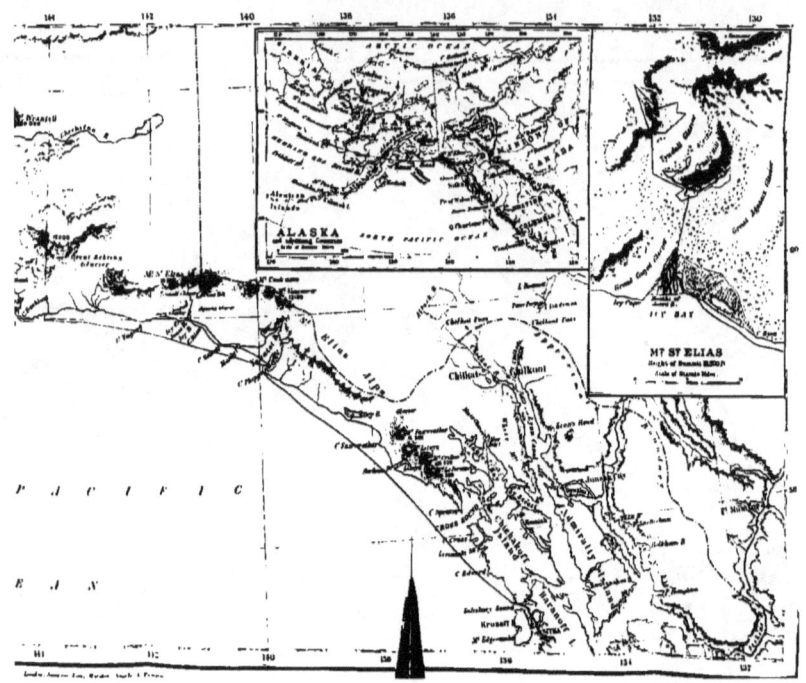

A Catalogue of American and Foreign Books Published or Imported by MESSRS. SAMPSON LOW & CO. can be had on application.

Crown Buildings, 188, Fleet Street, London,
October, 1886.

A Selection from the List of Books
PUBLISHED BY
SAMPSON LOW, MARSTON, SEARLE, & RIVINGTON.

ALPHABETICAL LIST.

ABBOTT (C. C.) Poaetquissings Chronicle: Upland and Meadow. 10s. 6d.

About Some Fellows. By an ETON BOY, Author of "A Day of my Life." Cloth limp, square 16mo, 2s. 6d.

Adams (C. K.) Manual of Historical Literature. Cr. 8vo, 12s. 6d.

Alcott (Louisa M.) Joe's Boys. 5s.

—— *Lulu's Library.* 3s. 6d.

—— *Old-Fashioned Thanksgiving Day.* 3s. 6d.

—— *Proverb Stories.* 16mo, 3s. 6d.

—— *Spinning-Wheel Stories.* 16mo, 5s.

—— See also "Rose Library."

Alden (W. L.) Adventures of Jimmy Brown, written by himself. Illustrated. Small crown 8vo, cloth, 2s. 6d.

Aldrich (T. B.) Friar Jerome's Beautiful Book, &c. Very choicely printed on hand-made paper, parchment cover, 3s. 6d.

—— *Poetical Works.* Édition de luxe. 8vo, 21s.

Alford (Lady Marian) Needlework as Art. With over 100 Woodcuts, Photogravures, &c. Royal 8vo, 42s.; large paper, 84s.

Amateur Angler's Days in Dove Dale: Three Weeks' Holiday in July and August, 1884. By E. M. Printed by Whittingham, at the Chiswick Press. Cloth gilt, 1s. 6d.; fancy boards, 1s.

American Men of Letters. Thoreau, Irving, Webster. 2s. 6d. each.

Andersen. Fairy Tales. With over 500 Illustrations by Scandinavian Artists. 6s. per vol.

Anderson (W.) Pictorial Arts of Japan. With 80 full-page and other Plates, 16 of them in Colours. Large imp. 4to, 8l. 8s. (in four folio parts, 2l. 2s. each); Artist's Proofs, 12l. 12s.

A

Angler's Strange Experiences (An). By COTSWOLD ISYS. With numerous Illustrations, 4to, 5s. New Edition, 3s. 6d.

Angling. See Amateur, "British Fisheries," "Cutcliffe," "Halford," "Hamilton," "Martin," "Orvis," "Pennell," "Pritt," "Stevens," "Theakston," "Walton," "Wells," and "Willis-Bund."

Arnold (Edwin) Birthday Book. 4s. 6d.

Art Education. See "Biographies of Great Artists," "Illustrated Text Books," "Mollett's Dictionary."

Artists at Home. Photographed by J. P. MAYALL, and reproduced in Facsimile. Letterpress by F. G. STEPHENS. Imp. folio, 42s.

Audsley (G. A.) Ornamental Arts of Japan. 90 Plates, 74 in Colours and Gold, with General and Descriptive Text. 2 vols., folio, £15 15s.; in specially designed leather, 23l. 2s.

—— *The Art of Chromo-Lithography.* Coloured Plates and Text. Folio, 63s.

Auerbach (B.) Brigitta. (B. Tauchnitz Collection.) 2s.
—— *On the Heights.* 3 vols., 6s.
—— *Spinoza.* 2 vols., 18mo, 4s.

BALDWIN (J.) Story of Siegfried. 6s.

—— *Story of Roland.* Crown 8vo, 6s.

Barlow (Alfred) Weaving by Hand and by Power. With several hundred Illustrations. Third Edition, royal 8vo, 1l. 5s.

Barrow (J.) Mountain Ascents in Cumberland and Westmoreland. 7s. 6d.

Bassett (F. S.) Legends and Superstitions of the Sea and of Sailors. 7s. 6d.

THE BAYARD SERIES.
Edited by the late J. HAIN FRISWELL.

Comprising Pleasure Books of Literature produced in the Choicest Style as Companionable Volumes at Home and Abroad.

"We can hardly imagine better books for boys to read or for men to ponder over."—*Times.*

Price 2s. 6d. each Volume, complete in itself, flexible cloth extra, gilt edges, with silk Headbands and Registers.

The Story of the Chevalier Bayard. By M. De Berville.	Abdallah; or, The Four Leaves. By Edouard Laboullaye.
De Joinville's St. Louis, King of France.	Table-Talk and Opinions of Napoleon Buonaparte.
The Essays of Abraham Cowley, including all his Prose Works.	Vathek: An Oriental Romance. By William Beckford.

Bayard Series (continued) :—

Words of Wellington : Maxims and Opinions of the Great Duke.
Dr. Johnson's Rasselas, Prince of Abyssinia. With Notes.
Hazlitt's Round Table. With Biographical Introduction.
The Religio Medici, Hydriotaphia, and the Letter to a Friend. By Sir Thomas Browne, Knt.
Coleridge's Christabel, and other Imaginative Poems. With Preface by Algernon C. Swinburne.
Lord Chesterfield's Letters, Sentences, and Maxims. With Introduction by the Editor, and Essay on Chesterfield by M. de Ste.-Beuve, of the French Academy.
Ballad Poetry of the Affections. By Robert Buchanan.
The King and the Commons. A Selection of Cavalier and Puritan Songs. Edited by Professor Morley.
Essays in Mosaic. By Thos. Ballantyne.
My Uncle Toby ; his Story and his Friends. Edited by P. Fitzgerald.
Reflections ; or, Moral Sentences and Maxims of the Duke de la Rochefoucauld.
Socrates : Memoirs for English Readers from Xenophon's Memorabilia. By Edw. Levien.
Prince Albert's Golden Precepts.

A Case containing 12 Volumes, price 31s. 6d.; or the Case separately, price 3s. 6d.

Behnke and Browne. Child's Voice. Small 8vo, 3s. 6d.

Beyschlag. Female Costume Figures of various Centuries. 12 designs in portfolio, imperial. 21s.

Bickersteth (Bishop E. H.) The Clergyman in his Home. Small post 8vo, 1s.

—— — *Evangelical Churchmanship and Evangelical Eclecticism.* 8vo, 1s.

—— — *From Year to Year : Original Poetical Pieces.* Small post 8vo, 3s. 6d. ; roan, 6s. and 5s.; calf or morocco, 10s. 6d.

—— — *Hymnal Companion to the Book of Common Prayer.* May be had in various styles and bindings from 1d. to 31s. 6d. Price List and Prospectus will be forwarded on application.

—— — The Master's Home-Call ; or, Brief Memorials of Alice Frances Bickersteth. 20th Thousand. 32mo, cloth gilt, 1s.

—— — The Master's Will. A Funeral Sermon preached on the Death of Mrs. S. Gurney Buxton. Sewn, 6d. ; cloth gilt, 1s.

—— — The Reef, and other Parables. Crown 8vo, 2s. 6d.

—— — The Shadow of the Rock. A Selection of Religious Poetry. 18mo, cloth extra, 2s. 6d.

—— — The Shadowed Home and the Light Beyond. New Edition, crown 8vo, cloth extra, 5s.

Biographies of the Great Artists (Illustrated). Crown 8vo, emblematical binding, 3s. 6d. per volume, except where the price is given.

Claude Lorrain.
Correggio, by M. E. Heaton, 2s. 6d.
Della Robbia and Cellini, 2s. 6d.
Albrecht Dürer, by R. F. Heath.
Figure Painters of Holland.
Fra Angelico, Masaccio, and Botticelli.
Fra Bartolommeo, Albertinelli, and Andrea del Sarto.
Gainsborough and Constable.
Ghiberti and Donatello, 2s. 6d.
Giotto, by Harry Quilter.
Hans Holbein, by Joseph Cundall.
Hogarth, by Austin Dobson.
Landseer, by F. G. Stevens.
Lawrence and Romney, by Lord Ronald Gower. 2s. 6d.
Leonardo da Vinci.
Little Masters of Germany, by W. B. Scott.
Mantegna and Francia.
Meissonier, by J. W. Mollett, 2s. 6d.
Michelangelo Buonarotti, by Clément.
Murillo, by Ellen E. Minor, 2s. 6d.
Overbeck, by J. B. Atkinson.
Raphael, by N. D'Anvers.
Rembrandt, by J. W. Mollett.
Reynolds, by F. S. Pulling.
Rubens, by C. W. Kett.
Tintoretto, by W. R. Osler.
Titian, by R. F. Heath.
Turner, by Cosmo Monkhouse.
Vandyck and Hals, by P. R. Head.
Velasquez, by E. Stowe.
Vernet and Delaroche, by J. Rees.
Watteau, by J. W. Mollett, 2s. 6d.
Wilkie, by J. W. Mollett.

Bird (F. J.) American Practical Dyer's Companion. 8vo, 42s.

Bird (H. E.) Chess Practice. 8vo, 2s. 6d.

Black (Robert) Horse Racing in France. 14s.

Black (Wm.) Novels. See "Low's Standard Library."

Blackburn (Charles F.) Hints on Catalogue Titles and Index Entries, with a Vocabulary of Terms and Abbreviations, chiefly from Foreign Catalogues. Royal 8vo, 14s.

Blackburn (Henry) Breton Folk. With 171 Illust. by RANDOLPH CALDECOTT. Imperial 8vo, gilt edges, 21s.; plainer binding, 10s. 6d.

—— *Pyrenees.* With 100 Illustrations by GUSTAVE DORÉ, corrected to 1881. Crown 8vo, 7s. 6d. See also CALDECOTT.

Blackmore (R. D.) Lorna Doone. Édition de luxe. Crown 4to, very numerous Illustrations, cloth, gilt edges, 31s. 6d.; parchment, uncut, top gilt, 35s.; new issue, plainer, 21s.; small post 8vo, 6s.

—— *Novels.* See "Low's Standard Library."

Blaikie (William) How to get Strong and how to Stay so. Rational, Physical, Gymnastic, &c., Exercises. Illust., sm. post 8vo, 5s.

—— *Sound Bodies for our Boys and Girls.* 16mo, 2s. 6d.

Bonwick. British Colonies. Asia, 1s.; Africa, 1s.; America, 1s.; Australasia, 1s. One vol., 5s.

Bosanquet (Rev. C.) Blossoms from the King's Garden: Sermons for Children. 2nd Edition, small post 8vo, cloth extra, 6s.

—— *Jehoshaphat; or, Sunlight and Clouds.* 1s.

Boulton (Major) North-West Rebellion in Canada. 9s.
Boussenard (L.) Crusoes of Guiana. Illustrated. 5s.
—— *Gold-seekers, a Sequel.* Illustrated. 16mo, 5s.
Bowker (R. R.) Copyright: its Law and its Literature. 15s.
Boyesen (F.) Story of Norway. 7s. 6d.
Boy's Froissart. King Arthur. Mabinogion. Percy. See LANIER.
Bradshaw (J.) New Zealand as it is. 8vo, 12s. 6d.
Brassey (Lady) Tahiti. With 31 Autotype Illustrations after Photos. by Colonel STUART-WORTLEY. Fcap. 4to, 21s.
Bright (John) Public Letters. Crown 8vo, 7s. 6d.
Brisse (Baron) Menus (366). A *ménu*, in French and English, for every Day in the Year. Translated by Mrs. MATTHEW CLARKE. 2nd Edition. Crown 8vo, 5s.
British Fisheries Directory, 1883-84. Small 8vo, 2s. 6d.
Brittany. See BLACKBURN.
Britons in Brittany. By G. H. F. 2s. 6d.
Brown. Life and Letters of John Brown, Liberator of Kansas, and Martyr of Virginia. By F. B. SANBORN. Illustrated. 8vo, 12s. 6d.
Browne (G. Lennox) Voice Use and Stimulants. Sm. 8vo, 3s. 6d.
—— *and Behnke (Emil) Voice, Song, and Speech.* Illustrated, 3rd Edition, medium 8vo, 15s.
Bryant (W. C.) and Gay (S. H.) History of the United States. 4 vols., royal 8vo, profusely Illustrated, 60s.
Bryce (Rev. Professor) Manitoba. With Illustrations and Maps. Crown 8vo, 7s. 6d.
Bunyan's Pilgrim's Progress. With 138 original Woodcuts. Small post 8vo, cloth gilt, 2s. 6d.; gilt edges, 3s.
Burnaby (Capt.) On Horseback through Asia Minor. 2 vols., 8vo, 38s. Cheaper Edition, 1 vol., crown 8vo, 10s. 6d.
Burnaby (Mrs. F.) High Alps in Winter; or, Mountaineering in Search of Health. By Mrs. FRED BURNABY. With Portrait of the Authoress, Map, and other Illustrations. Handsome cloth, 14s.
Butler (W. F.) The Great Lone Land; an Account of the Red River Expedition, 1869-70. New Edition, cr. 8vo, cloth extra, 7s. 6d.
—— *Invasion of England, told twenty years after, by an Old Soldier.* Crown 8vo, 2s. 6d.
—— *Red Cloud; or, the Solitary Sioux.* Imperial 16mo, numerous illustrations, gilt edges, 5s.
—— *The Wild North Land; the Story of a Winter Journey* with Dogs across Northern North America. 8vo, 18s. Cr. 8vo, 7s. 6d.

CADOGAN (*Lady A.*) *Illustrated Games of Patience.*
Twenty-four Diagrams in Colours, with Text. Fcap. 4to, 12s. 6d.
Caldecott (*Randolph*) *Memoir.* By HENRY BLACKBURN. With 170 (chiefly unpublished) Examples of the Artist's Work. 14s.; large paper, 21s.
California. See NORDHOFF.
Cambridge Staircase (*A*). By the Author of "A Day of my Life at Eton." Small crown 8vo, cloth, 2s. 6d.
Cambridge Trifles; from an Undergraduate Pen. By the Author of "A Day of my Life at Eton," &c. 16mo, cloth extra, 2s. 6d.
Campbell (*Lady Colin*) *Book of the Running Brook: and of Still Waters.* 5s.
Canadian People: Short History. Crown 8vo, 7s. 6d.
Carleton (*Will*) *Farm Ballads, Farm Festivals, and Farm Legends.* 1 vol., small post 8vo, 3s. 6d.
—— *City Ballads.* With Illustrations. 12s. 6d.
—— See also "Rose Library."
Carnegie (*A.*) *American Four-in-Hand in Britain.* Small 4to, Illustrated, 10s. 6d. Popular Edition, 1s.
—— *Round the World.* 8vo, 10s. 6d.
—— *Triumphant Democracy.* 6s.; also 1s. 6d. and 1s.
Chairman's Handbook (*The*). By R. F. D. PALGRAVE, Clerk of the Table of the House of Commons. 5th Edition, 2s.
Changed Cross (*The*), and other Religious Poems. 16mo, 2s. 6d.; calf or morocco, 6s.
Charities of London. See Low's.
Chattock (*R. S.*) *Practical Notes on Etching.* 8vo, 10s. 6d.
Chess. See BIRD (H. E.).
Children's Praises. Hymns for Sunday-Schools and Services. Compiled by LOUISA H. H. TRISTRAM. 4d.
Choice Editions of Choice Books. 2s. 6d. each. Illustrated by C. W. COPE, R.A., T. CRESWICK, R.A., E. DUNCAN, BIRKET FOSTER, J. C. HORSLEY, A.R.A., G. HICKS, R. REDGRAVE, R.A., C. STONEHOUSE, F. TAYLER, G. THOMAS, H. J. TOWNSHEND, E. H. WEHNERT, HARRISON WEIR, &c.

Bloomfield's Farmer's Boy.	Milton's L'Allegro.
Campbell's Pleasures of Hope.	Poetry of Nature. Harrison Weir.
Coleridge's Ancient Mariner.	Rogers' (Sam.) Pleasures of Memory.
Goldsmith's Deserted Village.	Shakespeare's Songs and Sonnets.
Goldsmith's Vicar of Wakefield.	Tennyson's May Queen.
Gray's Elegy in a Churchyard.	Elizabethan Poets.
Keat's Eve of St. Agnes.	Wordsworth's Pastoral Poems.

"Such works are a glorious beatification for a poet."—*Athenæum.*

Christ in Song. By PHILIP SCHAFF. New Ed., gilt edges, 6s.
Chromo-Lithography. See AUDSLEY.
Collingwood (Harry) Under the Meteor Flag. The Log of a Midshipman. Illustrated, small post 8vo, gilt, 6s.; plainer, 5s.
—— *The Voyage of the "Aurora."* Illustrated, small post 8vo, gilt, 6s.; plainer, 5s.
Composers. See "Great Musicians."
Cook (Dutton) Book of the Play. New Edition. 1 vol., 3s. 6d.
—— *On the Stage: Studies of Theatrical History and the Actor's Art.* 2 vols., 8vo, cloth, 24s.
Cowen (Jos., M.P.) Life and Speeches. By MAJOR JONES. 8vo, 14s.
Cozzens (F.) American Yachts. 27 Plates, 22 × 28 inches. Proofs, 21l.; Artist's Proofs, 31l. 10s.
Crown Prince of Germany: a Diary. 7s. 6d.
Cundall (Joseph) Annals of the Life and Work of Shakespeare. With a List of Early Editions. 3s. 6d.; large paper, 5s.
Cushing (W.) Initials and Pseudonyms: a Dictionary of Literary Disguises. Large 8vo, top edge gilt, 21s.
Custer (E. B.) Boots and Saddles. Life in Dakota with General Custer. Crown 8vo, 8s. 6d.
Cutcliffe (H. C.) Trout Fishing in Rapid Streams. Cr. 8vo, 3s. 6d.

D'ANVERS (N.) An Elementary History of Art. Crown 8vo, 10s. 6d.
—— *Elementary History of Music.* Crown 8vo, 2s. 6d.
—— *Handbooks of Elementary Art*—*Architecture; Sculpture; Old Masters; Modern Painting.* Crown 8vo, 3s. 6d. each.
Davis (Clement) Modern Whist. 4s.
Davis (C. T.) Manufacture of Bricks, Tiles, Terra-Cotta, &c. Illustrated. 8vo, 25s.
—— *Manufacture of Leather.* With many Illustrations. 52s. 6d.
—— *Manufacture of Paper.* 28s.
Dawidowsky (F.) Glue, Gelatine, Isinglass, Cements, &c. 8vo, 12s. 6d.
Day of My Life (A); or, Every-Day Experiences at Eton. By an ETON BOY. 16mo, cloth extra, 2s. 6d.
Day's Collacon: an Encyclopædia of Prose Quotations. Imperial 8vo, cloth, 31s. 6d.
Decoration. Vols. II. to XI. New Series, folio, 7s. 6d. each.

Dogs in Disease: their Management and Treatment. By ASH-MONT. Crown 8vo, 7s. 6d.

Donnelly (Ignatius) Atlantis; or, the Antediluvian World. 7th Edition, crown 8vo, 12s. 6d.

—— *Ragnarok: The Age of Fire and Gravel.* Illustrated, crown 8vo, 12s. 6d.

Doré (Gustave) Life and Reminiscences. By BLANCHE ROOSE-VELT. With numerous Illustrations from the Artist's previously unpublished Drawings. Medium 8vo, 24s.

Dougall (James Dalziel) Shooting: its Appliances, Practice, and Purpose. New Edition, revised with additions. Crown 8vo, 7s. 6d.

"The book is admirable in every way. . . . . We wish it every success."—*Globe*.
"A very complete treatise. . . . . Likely to take high rank as an authority on shooting."—*Daily News*.

Drama. See COOK (DUTTON).

Dyeing. See BIRD (F. J.).

Dunn (J. R.) Massacres of the Mountains: Indian Wars of the Far West. 21s.

Dupré (Giovanni). By H. S. FRIEZE. With Dialogues on Art by AUGUSTO CONTI. 7s. 6d.

*E*DUCATIONAL *List and Directory for* 1886-87. 5s.

Educational Works published in Great Britain. A Classified Catalogue. Second Edition, 8vo, cloth extra, 5s.

Egypt. See "Foreign Countries."

Eight Months on the Gran Chaco of the Argentine Republic. 8vo, 8s. 6d.

Electricity. See GORDON.

Elliott (H. W.) An Arctic Province: Alaska and the Seal Islands. Illustrated from Drawings; also with maps. 16s.

Ellis (W.) Royal Jubilees of England. 3s. 6d.

Emerson (Dr. P. H.) and Goodall. Life and Landscape on the Norfolk Broads. Plates 12 × 8 inches (before publication, 105s.), 126s.

Emerson (R. W.) Life. By G. W. COOKE. Crown 8vo, 8s. 6d.

English Catalogue of Books. Vol. III., 1872—1880 Royal 8vo, half-morocco, 42s. See also "Index."

English Etchings. A Periodical published Quarterly. 3s. 6d.

English Philosophers. Edited by E. B. IVAN MÜLLER, M.A.
A series intended to give a concise view of the works and lives of English thinkers. Crown 8vo volumes of 180 or 200 pp., price 3s. 6d. each.

Francis Bacon, by Thomas Fowler.
Hamilton, by W. H. S. Monck.
Hartley and James Mill, by G. S. Bower.

*John Stuart Mill, by Miss Helen Taylor.
Shaftesbury and Hutcheson, by Professor Fowler.
Adam Smith, by J. A. Farrer.

* *Not yet published.*

Etching. See CHATTOCK, and ENGLISH ETCHINGS.
Etchings (Modern) of Celebrated Paintings. 4to, 31s. 6d.

FARINI (G. A.) Through the Kalahari Desert: Fauna, Flora, and Strange Tribes. 21s.
Farm Ballads, Festivals, and Legends. See " Rose Library."
Fauriel (Claude) Last Days of the Consulate. Cr. 8vo, 10s. 6d.
Fawcett (Edgar) A Gentleman of Leisure. 1s.
Federighi. Seven Ages of Man. Lithographs from Drawings, 7 plates. 25s.
Feilden (H. St. C.) Some Public Schools, their Cost and Scholarships. Crown 8vo, 2s. 6d.
Fenn (G. Manville) Off to the Wilds: A Story for Boys. Profusely Illustrated. Crown 8vo, 7s. 6d. ; also 5s.
────── *The Silver Cañon: a Tale of the Western Plains.* Illustrated, small post 8vo, gilt, 6s.; plainer, 5s.
Fennell (Greville) Book of the Roach. New Edition, 12mo, 2s.
Ferns. See HEATH.
Field (H. M.) Greek Islands and Turkey after the War. 8s. 6d.
Fields (J. T.) Yesterdays with Authors. New Ed., 8vo, 10s. 6d.
Fitzgerald (Percy) Book Fancier: Romance of Book Collecting.
Fleming (Sandford) England and Canada: a Summer Tour. Crown 8vo, 6s.
Florence. See YRIARTE.
Folkard (R., Jun.) Plant Lore, Legends, and Lyrics. Illustrated. 8vo. 16s.

Forbes (H. O.) Naturalist's Wanderings in the Eastern Archipelago. Illustrated, 8vo, 21s.

Foreign Countries and British Colonies. A series of Descriptive Handbooks. Crown 8vo, 3s. 6d. each.

Australia, by J. F. Vesey Fitzgerald.
Austria, by D. Kay, F.R.G.S.
*Canada, by W. Fraser Rae.
Denmark and Iceland, by E. C. Otté.
Egypt, by S. Lane Poole, B.A.
France, by Miss M. Roberts
Germany, by S. Baring-Gould.
Greece, by L. Sergeant, B.A.
*Holland, by R. L. Poole.
Japan, by S. Mossman.
*New Zealand.
*Persia, by Major-Gen. Sir F. Goldsmid.
Peru, by Clements R. Markham, C.B.
Russia, by W. R. Morfill, M.A.
Spain, by Rev. Wentworth Webster.
Sweden and Norway, by F. H. Woods.
*Switzerland, by W. A. P. Coolidge, M.A.
*Turkey-in-Asia, by J. C. McCoan, M.P.
West Indies, by C. H. Eden, F.R.G.S.

* *Not ready yet.*

Fortnight in Heaven: an Unconventional Romance. 3s. 6d.

Fortunes made in Business. Vols. I., II., III. 16s. each.

Frampton (Mary) Journal, Letters, and Anecdotes, 1799—1846. 8vo, 14s.

Franc (Maud Jeanne). The following form one Series, small post 8vo, in uniform cloth bindings, with gilt edges :—

Emily's Choice. 5s.
Hall's Vineyard. 4s.
John's Wife : A Story of Life in South Australia. 4s.
Marian ; or, The Light of Some One's Home. 5s.
Silken Cords and Iron Fetters. 4s.
Into the Light. 4s.
Vermont Vale. 5s.
Minnie's Mission. 4s.
Little Mercy. 4s.
Beatrice Melton's Discipline. 4s.
No Longer a Child. 4s.
Golden Gifts. 4s.
Two Sides to Every Question. 4s.
Master of Ralston. 4s.

Frank's Ranche; or, My Holiday in the Rockies. A Contribution to the Inquiry into What we are to Do with our Boys. 5s.

French. See JULIEN.

Froissart. See LANIER.

Fuller (Edward) Fellow Travellers. 3s. 6d.

GALE (*F.; the Old Buffer*) *Modern English Sports: their Use and Abuse.* Crown 8vo, 6s.; a few large paper copies, 10s. 6d.

Galloway (W. B.) Chalk and Flint Formation. 2s. 6d.

Gane (D. N.) New South Wales and Victoria in 1885. 5s.
Geary (Grattan) Burma after the Conquest. 7s. 6d.
Gentle Life (Queen Edition). 2 vols. in 1, small 4to, 6s.

THE GENTLE LIFE SERIES.
Price 6s. each ; or in calf extra, price 10s. 6d. ; Smaller Edition, cloth extra, 2s. 6d., except where price is named.

The Gentle Life. Essays in aid of the Formation of Character of Gentlemen and Gentlewomen.

About in the World. Essays by Author of "The Gentle Life."

Like unto Christ. A New Translation of Thomas à Kempis' "De Imitatione Christi."

Familiar Words. An Index Verborum, or Quotation Handbook. 6s.

Essays by Montaigne. Edited and Annotated by the Author of "The Gentle Life."

The Gentle Life. 2nd Series.

The Silent Hour: Essays, Original and Selected. By the Author of "The Gentle Life."

Half-Length Portraits. Short Studies of Notable Persons. By J. HAIN FRISWELL.

Essays on English Writers, for the Self-improvement of Students in English Literature.

Other People's Windows. By J. HAIN FRISWELL. 6s.

A Man's Thoughts. By J. HAIN FRISWELL.

The Countess of Pembroke's Arcadia. By Sir PHILIP SIDNEY. New Edition, 6s.

George Eliot: a Critical Study of her Life. By G. W. COOKE. Crown 8vo, 10s. 6d.

Germany. By S. BARING-GOULD. Crown 8vo, 3s. 6d.

Gilder (W. H.) Ice-Pack and Tundra. An Account of the Search for the "Jeannette." 8vo, 18s.

—— *Schwatka's Search.* Sledging in quest of the Franklin Records. Illustrated, 8vo, 12s. 6d.

Gisborne (W.) New Zealand Rulers and Statesmen. With Portraits. Crown 8vo, 7s. 6d.

Gordon (General) Private Diary in China. Edited by S. MOSSMAN. Crown 8vo, 7s. 6d.

Gordon (J. E. H., B.A. Cantab.) Four Lectures on Electric Induction at the Royal Institution, 1878 9. Illust., square 16mo, 3s.

—— *Electric Lighting.* Illustrated, 8vo, 18s.

—— *Physical Treatise on Electricity and Magnetism.* 2nd Edition, enlarged, with coloured, full-page, &c., Illust. 2 vols., 8vo, 42s.

—— *Electricity for Schools.* Illustrated. Crown 8vo, 5s.

Gouffé (Jules) Royal Cookery Book. Translated and adapted for English use by ALPHONSE GOUFFÉ, Head Pastrycook to the Queen. New Edition, with plates in colours, Woodcuts, &c., 8vo gilt edges, 42s.

—— Domestic Edition, half-bound, 10s. 6d.

Grant (General, U.S.) Personal Memoirs. With numerous Illustrations, Maps, &c. 2 vols., 8vo, 28s.

Great Artists. See "Biographies."

Great Musicians. Edited by F. HUEFFER. A Series of Biographies, crown 8vo, 3s. each:—

Bach.	Handel.	Purcell.
*Beethoven.	Haydn.	Rossini.
*Berlioz.	*Marcello.	Schubert.
English Church Composers. By BARETT.	Mendelssohn.	Schumann.
	Mozart.	Richard Wagner.
*Gluck.	*Palestrina.	Weber.

* *In preparation.*

Greenwood (H.) Our Land Laws as they are. 2s. 6d.

Grimm (Hermann) Literature. 8s. 6d.

Groves (J. Percy) Charmouth Grange: a Tale of the Seven- teenth Century. Illustrated, small post 8vo, gilt, 6s.; plainer 5s.

Guizot's History of France. Translated by ROBERT BLACK. Super-royal 8vo, very numerous Full-page and other Illustrations. In 8 vols., cloth extra, gilt, each 24s. This work is re-issued in cheaper binding, 8 vols., at 10s. 6d. each.

"It supplies a want which has long been felt,' and ought to be in the hands of all students of history."—*Times.*

———————————— *Masson's School Edition.* Abridged from the Translation by Robert Black, with Chronological Index, Historical and Genealogical Tables, &c. By Professor GUSTAVE MASSON, B.A. With 24 full-page Portraits, and other Illustrations. 1 vol., 8vo, 600 pp., 10s. 6d.

Guyon (Mde.) Life. By UPHAM. 6th Edition, crown 8vo, 6s.

List of Publications. 13

HALFORD (*F. M.*) *Floating Flies, and how to Dress them.*
Coloured plates. 8vo, 15*s.*; large paper, 30*s.*

Hall (*W. W.*) *How to Live Long; or,* 1408 *Health Maxims,*
Physical, Mental, and Moral. 2nd Edition, small post 8vo, 2*s.*

Hamilton (*E.*) *Recollections of Fly-fishing for Salmon, Trout,*
and Grayling. With their Habits, Haunts, and History. Illustrated, small post 8vo, 6*s.*; large paper (100 numbered copies), 10*s.* 6*d.*

Hands (*T.*) *Numerical Exercises in Chemistry.* Cr. 8vo, 2*s.* 6*d.*
and 2*s.*; Answers separately, 6*d.*

Hardy (*Thomas*). See LOW'S STANDARD NOVELS.

Harland (*Marian*) *Home Kitchen: a Collection of Practical*
and Inexpensive Receipts. Crown 8vo, 5*s.*

Harley (*T.*) *Southward Ho! to the State of Georgia.* 5*s.*

Harper's Magazine. Published Monthly. 160 pages, fully
Illustrated, 1*s.* Vols., half yearly, I.—XII. (December, 1880, to November, 1886), super-royal 8vo, 8*s.* 6*d.* each.

"'Harper's Magazine' is so thickly sown with excellent illustrations that to count them would be a work of time; not that it is a picture magazine, for the engravings illustrate the text after the manner seen in some of our choicest *éditions de luxe*."—*St. James's Gazette.*
"It is so pretty, so big, and so cheap.... An extraordinary shillingsworth— 160 large octavo pages, with over a score of articles, and more than three times as many illustrations."—*Edinburgh Daily Review.*
"An amazing shillingsworth ... combining choice literature of both nations."— *Nonconformist.*

Harper's Young People. Vols. I.-II., profusely Illustrated with
woodcuts and 12 coloured plates. Royal 4to, extra binding, each 7*s.* 6*d.*; gilt edges, 8*s.* Published Weekly, in wrapper, 1*d.* 12mo. Annual Subscription, post free, 6*s.* 6*d.*; Monthly, in wrapper, with coloured plate, 6*d.*; Annual Subscription, post free, 7*s.* 6*d.*

Harrison (*Mary*) *Skilful Cook: a Practical Manual of Modern*
Experience. Crown 8vo, 5*s.*

Hatton (*Frank*) *North Borneo.* With Biography by JOSEPH
HATTON. New Map, and Illustrations, 18*s.*

Hatton (*Joseph*) *Journalistic London: with Engravings and*
Portraits of Distinguished Writers of the Day. Fcap. 4to, 12*s.* 6*d.*

—— *Three Recruits, and the Girls they left behind them.*
Small post 8vo, 6*s.*
"It hurries us along in unflagging excitement."—*Times.*

Heath (*Francis George*) *Fern World.* With Nature-printed
Coloured Plates. Crown 8vo, gilt edges, 12*s.* 6*d.* Cheap Edition, 6*s.*

Heldmann (Bernard) Mutiny on Board the Ship "Leander."
Small post 8vo, gilt edges, numerous Illustrations, 5s.
Henty (G. A.) Winning his Spurs. Illustrations. Cr. 8vo, 5s.
―― *Cornet of Horse : A Story for Boys.* Illust., cr. 8vo, 5s.
―― *Jack Archer : Tale of the Crimea.* Illust., crown 8vo, 5s.
―― *(Richmond) Australiana : My Early Life.* 5s.
Herrick (Robert) Poetry. Preface by AUSTIN DOBSON. With numerous Illustrations by E. A. ABBEY. 4to, gilt edges, 42s.
Hicks (E. S.) Our Boys : How to Enter the Merchant Service. 5s.
Higginson (T. W.) Larger History of the United States. 14s.
Hill (Staveley), Q.C., M.P.) From Home to Home : Two Long Vacations at the Foot of the Rocky Mountains. With Wood Engravings and Photogravures. 8vo, 21s.
Hitchman. Public Life of the Earl of Beaconsfield. 3s. 6d.
Hofmann. Scenes from the Life of our Saviour. 12 mounted plates, 12 × 9 inches, 21s.
Holder (C. F.) Marvels of Animal Life. 8s. 6d.
―― *Ivory King : the Elephant and its Allies.* Illustrated. 8s. 6d.
Holmes (O. Wendell) Poetical Works. 2 vols., 18mo, exquisitely printed, and chastely bound in limp cloth, gilt tops, 10s. 6d.
―― *Last Leaf : a Holiday Volume.* 42s.
―― *Mortal Antipathy.* 8s. 6d.
Homer, Iliad I.-XII., done into English Verse. By ARTHUR S. WAY. 9s.
―― *Odyssey.* Translated by A. S. WAY. 7s. 6d.
Hore (Mrs.) To Lake Tanganyika in a Bath Chair. Portraits and maps.
Hundred Greatest Men (The). 8 portfolios, 21s. each, or 4 vols., half-morocco, gilt edges, 10 guineas. New Ed., 1 vol., royal 8vo, 21s.
Hutchinson (T.) Diary and Letters. Vol. I., 16s. ; Vol. II., 16s.
Hygiene and Public Health. Edited by A. H. BUCK, M.D. Illustrated. 2 vols., royal 8vo, 42s.
Hymnal Companion of Common Prayer. See BICKERSTETH.

ILLUSTRATED Text-Books of Art-Education. Edited by EDWARD J. POYNTER, R.A. Each Volume contains numerous Illustrations, and is strongly bound for Students, price 5s. Now ready :—

PAINTING.

Classic and Italian. By PERCY R. HEAD.
German, Flemish, and Dutch.

French and Spanish.
English and American.

ARCHITECTURE.

Classic and Early Christian.
Gothic and Renaissance. By T. ROGER SMITH.

SCULPTURE.

Antique: Egyptian and Greek.
Renaissance and Modern. By LEADER SCOTT.

Index to the English Catalogue, Jan., 1874, *to Dec.,* 1880. Royal 8vo, half-morocco, 18s.

Indian Garden Series. See ROBINSON (PHIL.).

Irving (Henry) Impressions of America. By J. HATTON. 2 vols., 21s.; New Edition, 1 vol., 6s.

Irving (Washington). Complete Library Edition of his Works in 27 Vols., Copyright, Unabridged, and with the Author's Latest Revisions, called the "Geoffrey Crayon" Edition, handsomely printed in large square 8vo, on superfine laid paper. Each volume, of about 500 pages, fully Illustrated. 12s. 6d. per vol. *See also* "Little Britain."

——————— ("American Men of Letters.") 2s. 6d.

JAMES (C.) Curiosities of Law and Lawyers. 8vo, 7s. 6d

Japan. See ANDERSON, AUDSLEY, also MORSE.

Jerdon (Gertrude) Key-hole Country. Illustrated. Crown 8vo, cloth, 5s.

Johnston (H. H.) River Congo, from its Mouth to Bolobo. New Edition, 8vo, 21s.

Jones (Major) Heroes of Industry. Biographies with Portraits 7s. 6d.

——— *The Emigrants' Friend.* A Complete Guide to the United States. New Edition. 2s. 6d.

Julien (F.) English Student's French Examiner. 16mo, 2s.

——— *First Lessons in Conversational French Grammar.* Crown 8vo, 1s.

———*French at Home and at School.* Book I., Accidence, &c. Square crown 8vo, 2s.

Julien (F.) Conversational French Reader. 16mo, cloth, 2s. 6d
―――― *Petites Leçons de Conversation et de Grammaire.* 3s.
―――― *Phrases of Daily Use.* Limp cloth, 6d.
―――― *Petites Leçons and Phrases.* 3s. 6d.

KEMPIS (Thomas à) Daily Text-Book. Square 16mo, 2s. 6d.; interleaved as a Birthday Book, 3s. 6d.
Kent's Commentaries: an Abridgment for Students of American Law. By EDEN F. THOMPSON. 10s. 6d.
Kerr (W. M.) Far Interior: Cape of Good Hope, across the Zambesi, to the Lake Regions. Illustrated from Sketches, 2 vols. 8vo, 32s.
Kershaw (S. W.) Protestants from France in their English Home. Crown 8vo, 6s.
Kielland. Skipper Worsé. By the Earl of Ducie. Cr. 8vo, 10s. 6d.
Kingston (W. H. G.) Works. Illustrated, 16mo, gilt edges, 7s. 6d.; plainer binding, plain edges, 5s. each.
Heir of Kilfinnan. | Two Supercargoes.
Dick Cheveley. | With Axe and Rifle.
Snow-Shoes and Canoes. |
Kingsley (Rose) Children of Westminster Abbey: Studies in English History. 5s.
Knight (E. F.) Albania and Montenegro. Illust. 8vo, 12s. 6d.
Knight (E. J.) Cruise of the "Falcon." A Voyage to South America in a 30-Ton Yacht. Illust. New Ed. 2 vols., cr. 8vo, 24s.
Kunhardt. Small Yachts: Design and Construction. 35s.

LAMB (Charles) Essays of Elia. With over 100 designs by C. O. MURRAY. 6s.
Lanier's Works. Illustrated, crown 8vo, gilt edges, 7s. 6d. each.
Boy's King Arthur. | Boy's Percy: Ballads of Love and
Boy's Froissart. | Adventure, selected from the
Boy's Mabinogion; Original Welsh | "Reliques."
Legends of King Arthur. |
Lansdell (H.) Through Siberia. 2 vols., 8vo, 30s.; 1 vol., 10s. 6d.
―――― *Russia in Central Asia.* Illustrated. 2 vols, 42s.
Larden (W.) School Course on Heat. Second Edition, Illust. 5s.

Leonardo da Vinci's Literary Works. Edited by Dr. JEAN PAUL RICHTER. Containing his Writings on Painting, Sculpture, and Architecture, his Philosophical Maxims, Humorous Writings, and Miscellaneous Notes on Personal Events, on his Contemporaries, on Literature, &c. ; published from Manuscripts. 2 vols., imperial 8vo, containing about 200 Drawings in Autotype Reproductions, and numerous other Illustrations. Twelve Guineas.

Le Plongeon. Sacred Mysteries among the Mayas and the Quiches. 12s. 6d.

Library of Religious Poetry. Best Poems of all Ages. Edited by SCHAFF and GILMAN. Royal 8vo, 21s. ; cheaper binding, 10s. 6d.

Lindsay (W. S.) History of Merchant Shipping. Over 150 Illustrations, Maps, and Charts. In 4 vols., demy 8vo, cloth extra. Vols. 1 and 2, 11s. each ; vols. 3 and 4, 14s. each. 4 vols., 50s.

Little Britain, The Spectre Bridegroom, and *Legend of Sleeepy Hollow.* By WASHINGTON IRVING. An entirely New *Edition de luxe.* Illustrated by 120 very fine Engravings on Wood, by Mr. J. D. COOPER. Designed by Mr. CHARLES O. MURRAY. Re-issue, square crown 8vo, cloth, 6s.

Low's Standard Library of Travel and Adventure. Crown 8vo, uniform in cloth extra, 7s. 6d., except where price is given.
1. **The Great Lone Land.** By Major W. F. BUTLER, C.B.
2. **The Wild North Land.** By Major W. F. BUTLER, C.B.
3. **How I found Livingstone.** By H. M. STANLEY.
4. **Through the Dark Continent.** By H. M. STANLEY. 12s. 6d.
5. **The Threshold of the Unknown Region.** By C. R. MARKHAM. (4th Edition, with Additional Chapters, 10s. 6d.)
6. **Cruise of the Challenger.** By W. J. J. SPRY, R.N.
7. **Burnaby's On Horseback through Asia Minor.** 10s. 6d.
8. **Schweinfurth's Heart of Africa.** 2 vols., 15s.
9. **Marshall's Through America.**
10. **Lansdell's Through Siberia.** Illustrated and unabridged, 10s. 6d.

Low's Standard Novels. Small post 8vo, cloth extra, 6s. each, unless otherwise stated.
A Daughter of Heth. By W. BLACK.
In Silk Attire. By W. BLACK.
Kilmeny. A Novel. By W. BLACK.
Lady Silverdale's Sweetheart. By W. BLACK.
Sunrise. By W. BLACK.
Three Feathers. By WILLIAM BLACK.
Alice Lorraine. By R. D. BLACKMORE.
Christowell, a Dartmoor Tale. By R. D. BLACKMORE.
Clara Vaughan. By R. D. BLACKMORE.

Low's Standard Novels—continued.

Cradock Nowell. By R. D. BLACKMORE.
Cripps the Carrier. By R. D. BLACKMORE.
Erema; or, My Father's Sin. By R. D. BLACKMORE.
Lorna Doone. By R. D. BLACKMORE. 25th Edition.
Mary Anerley. By R. D. BLACKMORE.
Tommy Upmore. By R. D. BLACKMORE.
An English Squire. By Miss COLERIDGE.
Some One Else. By Mrs. B. M. CROKER.
A Story of the Dragonnades. By Rev. E. GILLIAT, M.A.
A Laodicean. By THOMAS HARDY.
Far from the Madding Crowd. By THOMAS HARDY.
Pair of Blue Eyes. By THOMAS HARDY.
Return of the Native. By THOMAS HARDY.
The Hand of Ethelberta. By THOMAS HARDY.
The Trumpet Major. By THOMAS HARDY.
Two on a Tower. By THOMAS HARDY.
Three Recruits. By JOSEPH HATTON.
A Golden Sorrow. By Mrs. CASHEL HOEY. New Edition.
Out of Court. By Mrs. CASHEL HOEY.
Don John. By JEAN INGELOW.
John Jerome. By JEAN INGELOW. 5s.
Sarah de Berenger. By JEAN INGELOW.
Adela Cathcart. By GEORGE MAC DONALD.
Guild Court. By GEORGE MAC DONALD.
Mary Marston. By GEORGE MAC DONALD.
Stephen Archer. New Ed. of "Gifts." By GEORGE MAC DONALD.
The Vicar's Daughter. By GEORGE MAC DONALD.
Weighed and Wanting. By GEORGE MAC DONALD.
Diane. By Mrs. MACQUOID.
Elinor Dryden. By Mrs. MACQUOID.
My Lady Greensleeves. By HELEN MATHERS.
Alaric Spenceley. By Mrs. J. H. RIDDELL.
Daisies and Buttercups. By Mrs. J. H. RIDDELL.
The Senior Partner. By Mrs. J. H. RIDDELL.
A Struggle for Fame. By Mrs. J. H. RIDDELL.
Jack's Courtship. By W. CLARK RUSSELL.
John Holdsworth. By W. CLARK RUSSELL.
A Sailor's Sweetheart. By W. CLARK RUSSELL.
Sea Queen. By W. CLARK RUSSELL.
Watch Below. By W. CLARK RUSSELL.
Strange Voyage. By W. CLARK RUSSELL.
Wreck of the Grosvenor. By W. CLARK RUSSELL.
The Lady Maud. By W. CLARK RUSSELL.
Little Loo. By W. CLARK RUSSELL.
The Late Mrs. Null. By FRANK R. STOCKTON.
My Wife and I. By Mrs. BEECHER STOWE.
Poganuc People, their Loves and Lives. By Mrs. B. STOWE.

Low's Standard Novels—continued.
 Ben Hur: a Tale of the Christ. By LEW. WALLACE.
 Anne. By CONSTANCE FENIMORE WOOLSON.
 East Angels. By CONSTANCE FENIMORE WOOLSON.
 For the Major. By CONSTANCE FENIMORE WOOLSON. 5s.
 French Heiress in her own Chateau.

Low's Handbook to the Charities of London. Edited and revised to date. Yearly, cloth, 1s. 6d.; paper, 1s.

M*CCORMICK (R.). Voyages of Discovery in the Arctic and Antarctic Seas in the "Erebus" and "Terror," in Search of Sir John Franklin, &c.* With Maps and Lithos. 2 vols., royal 8vo, 52s. 6d.

MacDonald (G.) Orts. Small post 8vo, 6s.
—— See also " Low's Standard Novels."

Mackay (Charles) New Glossary of Obscure Words in Shakespeare. 21s.

Macgregor (John) "Rob Roy" on the Baltic. 3rd Edition, small post 8vo, 2s. 6d.; cloth, gilt edges, 3s. 6d.

—— *A Thousand Miles in the "Rob Roy" Canoe.* 11th Edition, small post 8vo, 2s. 6d.; cloth, gilt edges, 3s. 6d.

—— *Voyage Alone in the Yawl "Rob Roy."* New Edition with additions, small post 8vo, 5s.; 3s. 6d. and 2s. 6d.

McLellan's Own Story: The War for the Union. Illustrations and maps. 18s.

Macquoid (Mrs.). See LOW'S STANDARD NOVELS.

Magazine. See DECORATION, ENGLISH ETCHINGS, HARPER.

Maginn (W.) Miscellanies. Prose and Verse. With Memoir. 2 vols., crown 8vo, 24s.

Main (Mrs.; Mrs. Fred Burnaby) High Life and Towers of Silence. Illustrated, square 8vo, 10s. 6d.

Manitoba. See BRYCE.

Manning (E. F.) Delightful Thames. Illustrated. 4to, fancy-boards, 5s.

Markham (C. R.) The Threshold of the Unknown Region. Crown 8vo, with Four Maps. 4th Edition. Cloth extra, 10s. 6d.

—— *War between Peru and Chili, 1879-1881.* Third Ed. Crown 8vo, with Maps, 10s. 6d.

—— See also "Foreign Countries."

Marshall (W. G.) Through America. New Ed., cr. 8vo, 7s. 6d.

Martin (J. W.) Float Fishing and Spinning in the Nottingham Style. New Edition. Crown 8vo, 2s. 6d.

Maury (Commander) Physical Geography of the Sea, and its Meteorology. New Edition, with Charts and Diagrams, cr. 8vo, 6s.

Men of Mark: a Gallery of Contemporary Portraits of the most Eminent Men of the Day, specially taken from Life. Complete in Seven Vols., 4to, handsomely bound, cloth, gilt edges, 25s. each.

Mendelssohn Family (The), 1729—1847. From Letters and Journals. Translated. New Edition, 2 vols., 8vo, 30s.

Mendelssohn. See also "Great Musicians."

Merrifield's Nautical Astronomy. Crown 8vo, 7s. 6d.

Merrylees (J.) Carlsbad and its Environs. 7s. 6d.; roan, 9s.

Mitchell (D. G.; Ik. Marvel) Works. Uniform Edition, small 8vo, 5s. each.

Bound together.
Doctor Johns.
Dream Life.
Out-of-Town Places.

Reveries of a Bachelor.
Seven Stories, Basement and Attic.
Wet Days at Edgewood.

Mitford (Mary Russell) Our Village. With 12 full-page and 157 smaller Cuts. Cr. 4to, cloth, gilt edges, 21s.; cheaper binding, 10s. 6d.

Milford (P.) Ned Stafford's Experiences in the United States. 5s.

Mollett (J. W.) Illustrated Dictionary of Words used in Art and Archæology. Terms in Architecture, Arms, Bronzes, Christian Art, Colour, Costume, Decoration, Devices, Emblems, Heraldry, Lace, Personal Ornaments, Pottery, Painting, Sculpture, &c. Small 4to, 15s.

Money (E.) The Truth about America. 5s.

Morley (H.) English Literature in the Reign of Victoria. 2000th volume of the Tauchnitz Collection of Authors. 18mo, 2s. 6d.

Morse (E. S.) Japanese Homes and their Surroundings. With more than 300 Illustrations. 21s.

Morwood. Our Gipsies in City, Tent, and Van. 8vo, 18s.

Moxley. Barbados, West Indian Sanatorium. 3s. 6d.

Muller (E.) Noble Words and Noble Deeds. 7s. 6d.; plainer binding, 5s.

Murray (E. C. Grenville) Memoirs. By his widow, COMTESSE DE RETHEL D'ARAGON.

Music. See "Great Musicians."

Mustard Leaves: Glimpses of London Society. By D.T.S. 3s. 6d.

NAPOLEON and Marie Louise: Memoirs. By Madame DURAND. 7s. 6d.

New Zealand. See BRADSHAW.

New Zealand Rulers and Statesmen. See GISBORNE.

Nicholls (J. H. Kerry) The King Country: Explorations in New Zealand. Many Illustrations and Map. New Edition, 8vo, 21s.

Nordhoff (C.) California, for Health, Pleasure, and Residence. New Edition, 8vo, with Maps and Illustrations, 12s. 6d.

Northbrook Gallery. Edited by LORD RONALD GOWER. 36 Permanent Photographs. Imperial 4to, 63s.; large paper, 105s.

Nott (Major) Wild Animals Photographed and Described. 35s.

Nursery Playmates (Prince of). 217 Coloured Pictures for Children by eminent Artists. Folio, in coloured boards, 6s.

O'BRIEN (R. B.) Fifty Years of Concessions to Ireland. With a Portrait of T. Drummond. Vol. I., 16s., II., 16s.

Orient Line Guide Book. By W. J. LOFTIE. 5s.

Orvis (C. F.) Fishing with the Fly. Illustrated. 8vo, 12s. 6d.

Our Little Ones in Heaven. Edited by the Rev. H. ROBBINS. With Frontispiece after Sir JOSHUA REYNOLDS. New Edition, 5s.

Outing: Magazine of Outdoor Sports. 1s. Monthly.

Owen (Douglas) Marine Insurance Notes and Clauses. New Edition, 14s.

PALLISER (Mrs.) A History of Lace. New Edition, with additional cuts and text. 8vo, 21s.

—— *The China Collector's Pocket Companion.* With upwards of 1000 Illustrations of Marks and Monograms. Small 8vo, 5s.

Pascoe (C. E.) London of To-Day. Illust., crown 8vo, 3s. 6d.

Payne (T. O.) Solomon's Temple and Capitol, Ark of the Flood and Tabernacle (four sections at 24s.), extra binding, 105s.

Pennell (H. Cholmondeley) Sporting Fish of Great Britain. 15s.; large paper, 30s.

Pharmacopœia of the United States of America. 8vo, 21s.

Philpot (H. J.) Diabetes Mellitus. Crown 8vo, 5s.

—— *Diet System.* Tables. I. Dyspepsia; II. Gout; III. Diabetes; IV. Corpulence. In cases, 1s. each.

Plunkett (Major G. T.) Primer of Orthographic Projection. Elementary Practical Solid Geometry clearly explained. With Problems and Exercises. Specially adapted for Science and Art Classes, and for Students who have not the aid of a Teacher. 2s.

Poe (E. A.) The Raven. Illustr. by DORÉ. Imperial folio, 63s.

Poems of the Inner Life. Chiefly from Modern Authors. Small 8vo, 5s.

Polar Expeditions. See GILDER, MARKHAM, MCCORMICK.

Porter (Noah) Elements of Moral Science. 10s. 6d.

Portraits of Celebrated Race-horses of the Past and Present Centuries, with Pedigrees and Performances. 31s. 6d. per vol.

Powell (W.) Wanderings in a Wild Country; or, Three Years among the Cannibals of New Britain. Illustr., 8vo, 18s.; cr. 8vo, 5s.

Poynter (Edward J., R.A.). See "Illustrated Text-books."

Pritt (T. E.) North Country Flies. Illustrated from the Author's Drawings. 10s. 6d.

Publishers' Circular (The), and General Record of British and Foreign Literature. Published on the 1st and 15th of every Month, 3d.

R*EBER (F.) History of Ancient Art.* 8vo, 18s.

Redford (G.) Ancient Sculpture. New edition. Crown 8vo, 10s. 6d.

Richter (Dr. Jean Paul) Italian Art in the National Gallery. 4to. Illustrated. Cloth gilt, 2l. 2s.; half-morocco, uncut, 2l. 12s. 6d.

—— See also LEONARDO DA VINCI.

Riddell (Mrs. J. H.) See LOW'S STANDARD NOVELS.

Robin Hood; Merry Adventures of. Written and illustrated by HOWARD PYLE. Imperial 8vo, 15s.

Robinson (Phil.) In my Indian Garden. Crown 8vo, limp cloth, 3s. 6d.

Robinson (Phil.) Indian Garden Series. 1s. 6d.; boards, 1s. each.
I. Chasing a Fortune, &c.: Stories. II. Tigers at Large. III. Valley of Teetotum Trees.

—— *Noah's Ark. A Contribution to the Study of Unnatural History.* Small post 8vo, 12s. 6d.

—— *Sinners and Saints: a Tour across the United States of America, and Round them.* Crown 8vo, 10s. 6d.

—— *Under the Punkah.* Crown 8vo, limp cloth, 5s.

Rockstro (W. S.) History of Music. New Edition. 8vo, 14s.

Rodrigues (J. C.) The Panama Canal. Crown 8vo, cloth extra, 5s.
"A series of remarkable articles . . . a mine of valuable data for editors and diplomatists."—*New York Nation.*

Roland: The Story of. Crown 8vo, illustrated, 6s.

Rome and the Environs. 3s.

Rose (J.) Complete Practical Machinist. New Ed., 12mo, 12s. 6d.

—— *Key to Engines and Engine Running.* 7s. 6d.

—— *Mechanical Drawing.* Illustrated, small 4to, 16s.

—— *Modern Steam Engines.* Illustrated. 31s. 6d.

Rose Library (The). Popular Literature of all Countries. Each volume, 1s. Many of the Volumes are Illustrated—

Little Women. By LOUISA M. ALCOTT.
Little Women Wedded. Forming a Sequel to "Little Women."
Little Women and Little Women Wedded. 1 vol., cloth gilt, 3s. 6d.
Little Men. By L. M. ALCOTT. Double vol., 2s.; cloth gilt, 3s. 6d.
An Old-Fashioned Girl. By LOUISA M. ALCOTT. 2s.; cloth, 3s. 6d.
Work. A Story of Experience. By L. M. ALCOTT. 3s. 6d.; 2 vols. 1s. each.
Stowe (Mrs. H. B.) The Pearl of Orr's Island.
—— **The Minister's Wooing.**
—— **We and our Neighbours.** 2s.; cloth gilt, 6s.
—— **My Wife and I.** 2s.; cloth gilt, 6s.
Hans Brinker; or, **the Silver Skates.** By Mrs. DODGE. Also 5s.

Rose Library (The)—continued.

My Study Windows. By J. R. LOWELL.
The Guardian Angel. By OLIVER WENDELL HOLMES.
My Summer in a Garden. By C. D. WARNER.
Dred. By Mrs. BEECHER STOWE. 2*s.*; cloth gilt, 3*s.* 6*d.*
Farm Ballads. By WILL CARLETON.
Farm Festivals. By WILL CARLETON.
Farm Legends. By WILL CARLETON.
Farm Ballads: Festivals and Legends. One vol., cloth, 3*s.* 6*d.*
The Clients of Dr. Bernagius. 3*s.* 6*d.*; 2 parts, 1*s.* each.
The Undiscovered Country. By W. D. HOWELLS. 3*s.* 6*d.* and 1*s.*
Baby Rue. By C. M. CLAY. 3*s.* 6*d.* and 1*s.*
The Rose in Bloom. By L. M. ALCOTT. 2*s.*; cloth gilt, 3*s.* 6*d.*
Eight Cousins. By L. M. ALCOTT. 2*s.*; cloth gilt, 3*s.* 6*d.*
Under the Lilacs. By L. M. ALCOTT. 2*s.*; also 3*s.* 6*d.*
Silver Pitchers. By LOUISA M. ALCOTT. Cloth, 3*s.* 6*d.*
Jemmy's Cruise in the "Pinafore," and other Tales. By LOUISA M. ALCOTT. 2*s.*; cloth gilt, 3*s.* 6*d.*
Jack and Jill. By LOUISA M. ALCOTT. 2*s.*; Illustrated, 5*s.*
Hitherto. By the Author of the "Gayworthys." 2 vols., 1*s.* each; 1 vol., cloth gilt, 3*s.* 6*d.*
A Gentleman of Leisure. A Novel. By EDGAR FAWCETT. 1*s.*
The Story of Helen Troy. 1*s.*

Ross (Mars) and Stonehewer Cooper. Highlands of Cantabria; or, Three Days from England. Illustrations and Map, 8vo, 21*s.*

Round the Yule Log: Norwegian Folk and Fairy Tales. Translated from the Norwegian of P. CHR. ASBJÖRNSEN. With 100 Illustrations after drawings by Norwegian Artists, and an Introduction by E. W. Gosse. Impl. 16mo, cloth extra, gilt edges, 7*s.* 6*d.* and 5*s.*

Rousselet (Louis) Son of the Constable of France. Small post 8vo, numerous Illustrations, 5*s.*

—— *King of the Tigers: a Story of Central India.* Illustrated. Small post 8vo, gilt, 6*s.*; plainer, 5*s.*

—— *Drummer Boy.* Illustrated. Small post 8vo, 5*s.*

Rowbotham (F.) Trip to Prairie Land. The Shady Side of Emigration. 5*s.*

Russell (W. Clark) *Jack's Courtship.* 3 vols., 31s. 6d.;
1 vol., 6s.

———— *The Lady Maud.* 3 vols., 31s. 6d.; 1 vol., 6s.

———— *Sea Queen.* 3 vols., 31s. 6d.; 1 vol., 6s.

———— *Strange Voyage.* 31s. 6d.

———— *Little Loo.* 6s.

———— *My Watch Below.* 6s.

———— *English Channel Ports and the Estate of the East and West India Dock Company.* Crown 8vo, 1s.

———— *Sailor's Language.* Illustrated. Crown 8vo, 3s. 6d.

———— *Wreck of the Grosvenor.* Small post 8vo, 6s.; 4to, sewed, 6d.

———— See also LOW's STANDARD NOVELS.

SAINTS *and their Symbols : A Companion in the Churches and Picture Galleries of Europe.* Illustrated. Royal 16mo, 3s. 6d.

Salisbury (Lord) *Life and Speeches.* By F. S. PULLING, M.A. With Photogravure Portrait of Lord Salisbury. 2 vols., cr. 8vo, 21s.

Sandilands (J. P.) *How to Develop Vocal Power.* 1s.

Saunders (A.) *Our Domestic Birds: Poultry in England and New Zealand.* Crown 8vo, 6s.

———— *Our Horses: the Best Muscles controlled by the Best Brains.* 6s.

Scherr (Prof. J.) *History of English Literature.* Cr. 8vo, 8s. 6d.

Schley. *Rescue of Greely.* Maps and Illustrations, 8vo, 12s. 6d.

Schuyler (Eugène) *American Diplomacy and the Furtherance of Commerce.* 12s. 6d.

———— *The Life of Peter the Great.* 2 vols., 8vo, 32s.

Schweinfurth (Georg) Heart of Africa. Three Years' Travels and Adventures in Unexplored Regions. 2 vols., crown 8vo, 15s.

Scott (Leader) Renaissance of Art in Italy. 4to, 31s. 6d.

—— *Sculpture, Renaissance and Modern.* 5s.

Senior (W.) Waterside Sketches. Imp. 32mo, 1s.6d., boards, 1s.

Shadbolt (S. H.) Afghan Campaigns of 1878—1880. By SYDNEY SHADBOLT. 2 vols., royal quarto, cloth extra, 3l.

Shakespeare. Edited by R. GRANT WHITE. 3 vols., crown 8vo, gilt top, 36s.; *édition de luxe*, 6 vols., 8vo, cloth extra, 63s.

Shakespeare. See also WHITE (R. GRANT).

Sidney (Sir Philip) Arcadia. New Edition, 6s.

Siegfried: The Story of. Illustrated, crown 8vo, cloth, 6s.

Simson (A.) Wilds of Ecuador and the Putumayor River. Crown 8vo.

Sinclair (Mrs.) Indigenous Flowers of the Hawaiian Islands. 44 Plates in Colour. Imp. folio, extra binding, gilt edges, 31s. 6d.

Sir Roger de Coverley. Re-imprinted from the "Spectator." With 125 Woodcuts and special steel Frontispiece. Small fcap. 4to, 6s.

Smith (G.) Assyrian Explorations and Discoveries. Illustrated by Photographs and Woodcuts. New Edition, demy 8vo, 18s.

—— *The Chaldean Account of Genesis.* With many Illustrations. 16s. New Ed. By PROFESSOR SAYCE. 8vo, 18s.

Smith (J. Moyr) Ancient Greek Female Costume. 112 full-page Plates and other Illustrations. Crown 8vo, 7s. 6d.

—— *Hades of Ardenne: The Caves of Han.* Crown 8vo, Illust., 5s.

—— *Legendary Studies, and other Sketches for Decorative Figure Panels.* 7s. 6d.

—— *Wooing of Æthra.* Illustrated. 32mo, 1s.

Smith (Sydney) Life and Times. By STUART J. REID. Illustrated. 8vo, 21s.

Smith (T. Roger) Architecture, Gothic and Renaissance. Illustrated, crown 8vo, 5s.

—————————————— *Classic and Early Christian.* 5s.

Smith (W. R.) Laws concerning Public Health. 8vo, 31s. 6d.

Spiers' French Dictionary. 29th Edition, remodelled. 2 vols., 8vo, 18s.; half bound, 21s.

Spry (W. J. J., R.N.) Cruise of H.M.S. "Challenger." With with Illustrations. 8vo, 18s. Cheap Edit., crown 8vo, 7s. 6d.

Spyri (Joh.) Heidi's Early Experiences: a Story for Children and those who love Children. Illustrated, small post 8vo, 4s. 6d.

———— *Heidi's Further Experiences.* Illust., sm. post 8vo, 4s. 6d.

Start (J. W. K.) Junior Mensuration Exercises. 8d.

Stanley (H. M.) Congo, and Founding its Free State. Illustrated, 2 vols., 8vo, 42s.; re-issue, 2 vols. 8vo, 21s.

———— *How I Found Livingstone.* 8vo, 10s. 6d.; cr. 8vo, 7s. 6d.

———— *Through the Dark Continent.* Crown 8vo, 12s. 6d.

Stenhouse (Mrs.) An Englishwoman in Utah. Crown 8vo, 2s. 6d.

Sterry (J. Ashby) Cucumber Chronicles. 5s.

Stevens (E. W.) Fly-Fishing in Maine Lakes. 8s. 6d.

Stewart's Year Book of New Zealand, 1886-87. 7s. 6d.

Stockton (Frank R.) The Story of Viteau. Illust. Cr. 8vo, 5s.

———— *The Late Mrs. Null.* Crown 8vo, 6s.

Stoker (Bram) Under the Sunset. Crown 8vo, 6s.

Stowe (Mrs. Beecher) Dred. Cloth, gilt edges, 3s. 6d.; boards, 2s.

———— *Little Foxes.* Cheap Ed., 1s.; Library Edition, 4s. 6d.

———— *My Wife and I.* 6s.

———— *Old Town Folk.* 6s.; also 3s.

———— *Old Town Fireside Stories.* Cloth extra, 3s. 6d.

———— *We and our Neighbours.* 6s.

Stowe (Mrs. Beecher) Poganuc People. 6s.

—— —— *Chimney Corner.* 1s.; cloth, 1s. 6d.

—— —— See also ROSE LIBRARY.

Stuttfield (Hugh E. M.) El Maghreb: 1200 *Miles' Ride through Marocco.* 8s. 6d.

Sullivan (A. M.) Nutshell History of Ireland. Paper boards, 6d.

Sutton (A. K.) A B C Digest of the Bankruptcy Law. 8vo, 3s. and 2s. 6d.

TAINE (H. A.) "Les Origines de la France Contemporaine." Translated by JOHN DURAND.
    I. The Ancient Regime. Demy 8vo, cloth, 16s.
    II. The French Revolution. Vol. 1. do.
    III. Do. do. Vol. 2. do.
    IV. Do. do. Vol. 3. do.

Talbot (Hon. E.) A Letter on Emigration. 1s.

Tauchnitz's English Editions of German Authors. Each volume, cloth flexible, 2s.; or sewed, 1s. 6d. (Catalogues post free.)

Tauchnitz (B.) German Dictionary. 2s.; paper, 1s. 6d.; roan, 2s. 6d.

—— —— *French Dictionary.* 2s.; paper, 1s. 6d.; roan, 2s. 6d.

—— —— *Italian Dictionary.* 2s.; paper, 1s. 6d.; roan, 2s. 6d.

—— —— *Latin Dictionary.* 2s.; paper, 1s. 6d.; roan, 2s. 6d.

—— —— *Spanish and English.* 2s.; paper, 1s. 6d.; roan, 2s. 6d.

—— —— *Spanish and French.* 2s.; paper, 1s. 6d.; roan, 2s. 6d.

Taylor (R. L.) Chemical Analysis Tables. 1s.

Taylor (W. M.) Joseph the Prime Minister. 6s.

—— —— *Paul the Missionary.* Crown 8vo, 7s. 6d.

Techno-Chemical Receipt Book. With additions by BRANNT and WAHL. 10s. 6d.

Thausing (Prof.) Malt and the Fabrication of Beer. 8vo, 45s.

Theakston (M.) British Angling Flies. Illustrated. Cr. 8vo, 5s.

Thomson (Jos.) Through Masai Land. Illust. and Maps. 21s.

Thomson (W.) Algebra for Colleges and Schools. With Answers, 5s. ; without, 4s. 6d. ; Answers separate, 1s. 6d.

Thoreau. American Men of Letters. Crown 8vo, 2s. 6d.

Tissandier, Photography. Edited by J. THOMSON, with Appendix by H. FOX TALBOT. Illustrated. 6s.

Tolhausen. Supplément du Dictionnaire Technologique. 3s. 6d.

Tristram (Rev. Canon) Pathways of Palestine. Series I., with Permanent Photographs. 2 vols.,folio, cloth, gilt edges, 31s. 6d. each.

Trollope (Anthony) Thompson Hall. 1s.

Tromholt (S.) Under the Rays of the Aurora Borealis. By C. SIEWERS. Photographs and Portraits. 2 vols., 8vo, 30s.

Tucker (W. J.) Life and Society in Eastern Europe. 15s.

Tupper (Martin Farquhar) My Life as an Author. 14s.

Turner (Edward) Studies in Russian Literature. Cr. 8vo, 8s. 6d.

UNION Jack (The). Every Boy's Paper. Edited by G. A. HENTY. Profusely Illustrated with Coloured and other Plates. Vol. I., 6s. Vols. II., III., IV., 7s. 6d. each.

VALLANCE (Lucy) Paul's Birthday. 3s. 6d.

Van Kampen (S. R.) Nicholas Godfried Van Kampen: a Biographical Sketch By SAMUEL R. VAN CAMPEN. 14s.

Vasili (Count) Berlin Society. Translated. Cr. 8vo, 6s.

—— *World of London (La Société de Londres).* Cr. 8vo, 6s.

Victoria (Queen) Life of. By GRACE GREENWOOD. Illust. 6s.

Vincent (Mrs. Howard) Forty Thousand Miles over Land and Water. With Illustrations. New Edti., 3s. 6d.

Viollet-le-Duc (E.) Lectures on Architecture. Translated by BENJAMIN BUCKNALL, Architect. With 33 Steel Plates and 200 Wood Engravings. Super-royal 8vo, leather back, gilt top, 2 vols., 3l. 3s.

BOOKS BY JULES VERNE.

WORKS.	Large Crown 8vo. Containing 350 to 600 pp. and from 50 to 100 full-page illustrations.		Containing the whole of the text with some illustrations.	
	In very handsome cloth binding, gilt edges.	In plainer binding, plain edges.	In cloth binding, gilt edges, smaller type.	Coloured boards.
	s. d.	s. d.	s. d.	
20,000 Leagues under the Sea. Parts I. and II.	10 6	5 0	3 6	2 vols., 1s. each.
Hector Servadac	10 6	5 0	3 6	2 vols., 1s. each.
The Fur Country	10 6	5 0	3 6	2 vols., 1s. each.
The Earth to the Moon and a Trip round it	10 6	5 0	2 vols., 2s. ea.	2 vols., 1s. each.
Michael Strogoff	10 6	5 0	3 6	2 vols., 1s. each.
Dick Sands, the Boy Captain	10 6	5 0	3 6	2 vols., 1s. each.
Five Weeks in a Balloon	7 6	3 6	2 0	1s. 0d.
Adventures of Three Englishmen and Three Russians	7 6	3 6	2 0	1 0
Round the World in Eighty Days	7 6	3 6	2 0	1 0
A Floating City	7 6	3 6	2 0	1 0
The Blockade Runners			2 0	1 0
Dr. Ox's Experiment	—	—	2 0	1 0
A Winter amid the Ice	—	—	2 0	1 0
Survivors of the "Chancellor"	7 6	3 6	3 6	2 vols., 1s. each.
Martin Paz			2 0	1s. 0d.
The Mysterious Island, 3 vols.: —	22 6	10 6	6 0	3 0
I. Dropped from the Clouds	7 6	3 6	2 0	1 0
II. Abandoned	7 6	3 6	2 0	1 0
III. Secret of the Island	7 6	3 6	2 0	1 0
The Child of the Cavern	7 6	3 6	2 0	1 0
The Begum's Fortune	7 6	3 6	2 0	1 0
The Tribulations of a Chinaman	7 6	3 6	2 0	1 0
The Steam House, 2 vols.:—				
I. Demon of Cawnpore	7 6	3 6	2 0	1 0
II. Tigers and Traitors	7 6	3 6	2 0	1 0
The Giant Raft, 2 vols.:—				
I. 800 Leagues on the Amazon	7 6	3 6	2 0	1 0
II. The Cryptogram	7 6	3 6	2 0	1 0
The Green Ray	6 0	5 0	—	1 0
Godfrey Morgan	7 6	3 6	2 0	1 0
Kéraban the Inflexible:—				
I. Captain of the "Guidara"	7 6	3 6		
II. Scarpante the Spy	7 6	3 6		
The Archipelago on Fire	7 6			
The Vanished Diamond	7 6			
Mathias Sandorf	10 6			
Lottery Ticket	7 6			

CELEBRATED TRAVELS AND TRAVELLERS. 3 vols. 8vo, 600 pp., 100 full-page illustrations, 12s. 6d.; gilt edges, 14s. each:—(1) THE EXPLORATION OF THE WORLD. (2) THE GREAT NAVIGATORS OF THE EIGHTEENTH CENTURY. (3) THE GREAT EXPLORERS OF THE NINETEENTH CENTURY.

W*AHL* (*W. H.*) *Galvanoplastic Manipulation for the* Electro-Plater. 8vo, 35s.
Wakefield. Aix-les-Bains: Bathing and Attractions. 2s. 6d.
Wallace (*L.*) *Ben Hur: A Tale of the Christ.* Crown 8vo, 6s.
Waller (*Rev. C. H.*) *The Names on the Gates of Pearl,* and other Studies. New Edition. Crown 8vo, cloth extra, 3s. 6d.
—— *A Grammar and Analytical Vocabulary of the Words in* the Greek Testament. Compiled from Brüder's Concordance. Part I. Grammar. Small post 8vo, cloth, 2s. 6d. Part II. Vocabulary, 2s. 6d.
—— *Adoption and the Covenant.* On Confirmation. 2s. 6d.
—— *Silver Sockets; and other Shadows of Redemption.* Sermons at Christ Church, Hampstead. Small post 8vo, 6s.
Walton (*Iz.*) *Wallet Book*, ClƆIƆLXXXV. 21s.; l.p. 42s.
—— (*T. H.*) *Coal Mining.* With Illustrations. 4to, 25s.
Warner (*C. D.*) *My Summer in a Garden.* Boards, 1s.; leatherette, 1s. 6d.; cloth, 2s.
Warren (*W. F.*) *Paradise Found; the North Pole the Cradle* of the Human Race. Illustrated. Crown 8vo, 12s. 6d.
Washington Irving's Little Britain. Square crown 8vo, 6s.
Watson (*P. B.*) *Marcus Aurelius Antoninus.* 8vo, 15s.
Webster. ("American Men of Letters.") 18mo, 2s. 6d.
Weir (*Harrison*) *Animal Stories, Old and New,* told in Pictures and Prose. Coloured, &c., Illustrations. 56 pp., 4to, 5s.
Wells (*H. P.*) *American Salmon Fisherman.* 6s.
—— *Fly Rods and Fly Tackle.* Illustrated. 10s. 6d.
—— (*J. W.*) *Three Thousand Miles through Brazil.* Illustrated from Original Sketches. 2 vols. 8vo, 32s.
Wheatley (*H. B.*) *and Delamotte* (*P. H.*) *Art Work in Porcelain.* Large 8vo, 2s. 6d.
—— *Art Work in Gold and Silver. Modern.* 2s. 6d.
—— *Handbook of Decorative Art.* 10s. 6d.
Whisperings. Poems. Small post 8vo, gilt edges, 3s. 6d.
White (*R. Grant*) *England Without and Within.* Crown 8vo, 10s. 6d.
—— *Every-day English.* 10s. 6d. Words, &c.
—— *Fate of Mansfield Humphreys, the Episode of Mr.* Washington Adams in England, an Apology, &c. Crown 8vo, 6s.
—— *Studies in Shakespeare.* 10s. 6d.
—— *Words and their Uses.* New Edit., crown 8vo, 5s.
Whittier (*J. G.*) *The King's Missive, and later Poems.* 18mo, choice parchment cover, 3s. 6d.

Whittier (J. G.) The Whittier Birthday Book. Uniform with the "Emerson Birthday Book." Square 16mo, very choice binding, 3s. 6d.
—— *Life of.* By R. A. UNDERWOOD. Cr. 8vo, cloth, 10s. 6d.
—— *St. Gregory's Guest, &c.* Recent Poems. 5s.
Williams (C. F.) Tariff Laws of the United States. 8vo, 10s. 6d.
—— *(H. W.) Diseases of the Eye.* 8vo, 21s.
Wills, A Few Hints on Proving, without Professional Assistance. By a PROBATE COURT OFFICIAL. 8th Edition, revised, with Forms of Wills, Residuary Accounts, &c. Fcap. 8vo, cloth limp, 1s.
Wills (Dr. C. J.) Persia as it is. Crown 8vo.
Willis-Bund (J.) Salmon Problems. 3s. 6d.; boards, 2s. 6d.
Wilson (Dr. Andrew) Health for the People.
Wimbledon (Viscount) Life and Times, 1628-38. By C. DALTON. 2 vols., 8vo, 30s.
Winsor (Justin) Narrative and Critical History of America. 8 vols., 30s. each; large paper, per vol., 63s.
Witthaus (R. A.) Medical Student's Chemistry. 8vo, 16s.
Woodbury, History of Wood Engraving. Illustrated. 8vo, 18s.
Woolsey. Introduction to International Law. 5th Ed., 18s.
Woolson (Constance F.) See "Low's Standard Novels."
Wright (H.) Friendship of God. Portrait, &c. Crown 8vo, 6s.
Wright (T.) Town of Cowper, Olney, &c. 6s.
Written to Order; the Journeyings of an Irresponsible Egotist. By the Author of "A Day of my Life at Eton." Crown 8vo, 6s.

YRIARTE *(Charles) Florence: its History.* Translated by C. B. PITMAN. Illustrated with 500 Engravings. Large imperial 4to, extra binding, gilt edges, 63s.; or 12 Parts, 5s. each.
History; the Medici; the Humanists; letters; arts; the Renaissance; illustrious Florentines; Etruscan art; monuments; sculpture; painting.

London:
SAMPSON LOW, MARSTON, SEARLE, & RIVINGTON,
CROWN BUILDINGS, 188, FLEET STREET, E.C.

www.ingramcontent.com/pod-product-compliance
Lightning Source LLC
Chambersburg PA
CBHW032053220426
43664CB00008B/981